Study Guide and Workbook
for Spiritual and Church Renewal

Study Guide and Workbook for Spiritual and Church Renewal

Companion to the *Handbook for the Christian Faith*

James M. Dawsey,
Sharon E. Wright,
and Scott Sikes

CASCADE *Books* • Eugene, Oregon

STUDY GUIDE AND WORKBOOK FOR SPIRITUAL AND CHURCH RENEWAL
Companion to the *Handbook for the Christian Faith*

Copyright © 2025 James M. Dawsey, Sharon E. Wright, and Scott Sikes. All rights reserved. Except for brief quotations in critical publications or reviews, no part of this book may be reproduced in any manner without prior written permission from the publisher. Write: Permissions, Wipf and Stock Publishers, 199 W. 8th Ave., Suite 3, Eugene, OR 97401.

Cascade Books
An Imprint of Wipf and Stock Publishers
199 W. 8th Ave., Suite 3
Eugene, OR 97401

www.wipfandstock.com

PAPERBACK ISBN: 978-1-6667-8460-2
HARDCOVER ISBN: 978-1-6667-8461-9
EBOOK ISBN: 978-1-6667-8462-6

Cataloguing-in-Publication data:

Names: Dawsey, James M., author. | Wright, Sharon E., author. | Sikes, Scott, author.

Title: Study guide and workbook for spiritual and church renewal : companion to the *Handbook for the Christian Faith* / James M. Dawsey, Sharon E. Wright, and Scott Sikes.

Description: Eugene, OR : Cascade Books, 2025 | Includes bibliographical references.

Identifiers: ISBN 978-1-6667-8460-2 (paperback) | ISBN 978-1-6667-8461-9 (hardcover) | ISBN 978-1-6667-8462-6 (ebook)

Subjects: LCSH: Methodist Church—Doctrines—History. | Methodist Church—Doctrines. | Methodist Church—United States—Doctrines.

Classification: BX8331.2 .D37 2025 (paperback) | BX8331.2 .D37 (ebook)

VERSION NUMBER 02/04/25

Scripture quotations are from the New Revised Standard Version of the Bible (NRSV), copyright © 1989 National Council of Churches of Christ in the United States of America. Used by permission. All rights reserved worldwide.

"The fear of the Lord is the beginning of knowledge." (Prov 1:7)

Contents

Preface | ix
Acknowledgments | xi

Introduction: We've Reached a Changing Point | 1

1. The Human Condition | 9
2. Understanding God's Commandments | 16
3. Repentance and Grace | 24
4. Conversion? | 31
5. Religion Itself: Progressing in Holiness | 39
6. Pietism | 47
7. The Scriptures | 55
8. Church History, Reason, and Christian Experience: Natural Theology | 63
9. The History of Methodist Women | 71
10. The Ideal of Equality and History of Racism | 81
11. The LGBTQ+ Community | 91
12. Evangelism and the Great Awakening | 99
13. Missions | 108
14. Church and World: Doing Good | 117
15. The Church as Church: The Nature and Institutional Structure of the Church, Church Governance, and Organization | 126

Conclusion: An Agenda for Contemporary Methodists and Like-Minded Protestants | 135

Preface

THIS STUDY GUIDE WORKBOOK is designed to accompany James M. Dawsey's *Handbook for the Christian Faith: Essential Beliefs and Practices for Twenty-first Century American Methodists and Like-minded Protestants: A Book about Extraordinary People*, with primary use in Emory & Henry University's certification course on Spiritual and Church Renewal. For each chapter of the textbook, the study guide offers an overview and summary of content; identifies significant terms, names, dates, and events of the history being recounted; lists and defines important themes and materials to be learned; provides exercises to aid learning and enhance understanding; and offers a bibliography of pertinent readings.

Questions are designed to engage participants in a detailed reading of the text and in reviewing lecture notes. After reading the text and working through the materials in the study guide, participants will be well equipped to complete certification requirements.

The certification course is appropriate for religious professionals who wish perhaps to reexamine and enhance their understanding of the Christian faith. There are practical aspects to being credentialed, important to those following a religious vocation. And certification can likewise prove a significant career step for the curious from other professions—historians, sociologists, writers, pundits, and researchers—who wish to understand the grip Christianity has exerted on Western culture and history and also to decipher the chaos of present-day American Christianity.

But besides these professionals, most often the course will be peopled by church groups reading the *Handbook for the Christian Faith* and discussing the issues raised within it, attempting to discern a right path for contemporary Christianity and their local congregations. The course in Spiritual and Church Renewal encourages group study. But while there is a community focus to the course, true spiritual and church renewal begins with individuals. Participants will come from different backgrounds and hold various motives for certification. There are those associated by birth with the church, who have drifted away yet long to be reunited with the deeper meaning of Christianity. There are some searching for something lost, wishing for a stronger bond with their creator. There are seekers attracted to the Christian philosophy of living an other-directed life, those searching for happiness and fulfillment, and those who want to change the world for the better. And others' sole purpose will be to reflect more deeply on the meaning of the Christian heritage.

The exercises in this workbook extend beyond understanding Christianity as a religion to participants better understanding themselves as Christians. What are the steps to becoming more faithful Christians? And what marks will identify Methodists and like-minded Protestants in this century?

So, let's enter into our study as church groups and individuals purposing to reflect more deeply on the meaning of the Christian heritage.

Acknowledgments

THE AUTHORS EXPRESS GRATITUDE to Dr. Michael Puglisi and the administrative staff of the Offices of the Provost and Academic Affairs, Spiritual Life, and the Appalachian Center for Civic Life; the librarians and staff of the Frederick Thrasher Kelly Library; and the director and technical staff of Online Education at Emory & Henry.

Introduction

We've Reached a Changing Point

Overview and Summary of Content

The Opening Problem

THE HANDBOOK FOR THE *Christian Faith* textbook introduces its subject by pointing out the diminishing influence of Christianity in American life. Among the evidence are Gallup, Public Religion Institute, Pew Forum on Religion and Public Life, and General Social Survey polls showing significant declines in church membership, trending increase among respondents identifying themselves as "nones" when asked about religious affiliation, and pervasive ignorance concerning basic Christian history, beliefs, and practices. Incomprehension extends not only to the general American public but to those claiming to be adherents. Statistical evidence also points to the aging Christian congregations with the young being the most conspicuously absent from the pews. While the pre-COVID median age in our American population was thirty-five, the median age of attendees at Sunday worship in the largest of the Methodist denominations was fifty-seven—and that median age proves even older in some other churches.

But the *Handbook* expresses deeper concerns than the shrinking membership of Methodists and similar Protestant denominations. The values of society are in large measure molded by religion. What will become the shape of Protestant Christianity emerging in the twenty-first century? And of Methodism? And beyond that, what kind of community will the United States of America be?

Rediscovering Roots

The introductory chapter reminds us that times of crisis often paradoxically present opportunities. And the author suggests that Christianity will thrive if Christians are true to their religious roots; if they focus on Christ's priorities and don't shy away from the work necessary to meet them; if they let the mind of Christ hold sway over their own way of thinking; if they focus on the church as a community, the body of Christ, instead of an aggregate of individuals; and if guided by the Holy Spirit, they exhibit the persistence and the creativity expected of followers of Christ.

Rediscovering the deep roots of the Christian faith will not be an easy task. Culture can corrupt religion. The desire for power and wealth may color religion with hypocrisy. Churches face challenges of misstatement and misinterpretation, often because of ignorance. But sometimes the misrepresentations are purposeful. We are reminded not to ignore human frailty. There are many Christianities, so to speak. The text uses the metaphor of a large river for Christianity, asking participants to reflect on whether their religion has come untied from its moorings. Are they holding beliefs and practices essential to the Christian faith? When might Christians be navigating in deep water, and when might they be drifting in the weeds? These are appropriate questions for church groups and individuals to ask themselves.

Reasons for American Christianity's Unhealthiness

The introductory chapter of the *Handbook* emphasizes that a vast majority of American churchgoers are well-meaning people of faith trying each day to live a moral life, wanting to be followers of Christ. A principal reason that Christians are unclear about the essential beliefs and practices of their faith is that they live busy lives with ever-decreasing time set aside for religious study, reflection, and meditation. There is no substitute for time on task if Christians are to be better informed about their faith and if the experience of religion is to play a larger role in their lives. But, there are other reasons why people brought up in the Christian faith might have lost touch with their religious roots: opportunities for service outside the church in charitable organizations, the politicization of everything including churches in our society, urbanization with the accompanying loss of a home church, the lessened involvement of the extended family in the lives of the young, the decrease in the size of the nuclear family, and such are mentioned in passing.

The author then turns attention to two reasons peculiar to the development of American religion for American Protestantism's loss of roots.

The first is the voluntarism of American religious affiliation. Historically, adherents have joined religious fellowships where they felt at home, where there were like-minded and like-hearted individuals. The act of joining was often simple, requiring little from the new member. Sometimes there was an added stipulation of a short course of study or catechism.

While on balance a liberating force, voluntarism led to a sameness in church congregations as adherents selected to worship alongside people who were socially, economically, racially, and politically like them. Voluntarism also produced a marketplace quality to American Protestantism as churches competed for "customers." The marketplace, unfortunately, affected ministers as they succumbed to pressures of membership and budget. A premium was placed on preachers who have honed their persuasive abilities. With the development of megachurches, rigorous theological training and pastoral concern took a backseat to showmanship and psychological persuasion. Is it surprising that ministers who receive salaries in line with the CEOs of successful companies sometimes bend to pressure and moderate the prophetic voice from the pulpit?

The second reason peculiar to American Protestantism's loss of roots raised by the *Handbook*'s author concerns the religion's spread through awakenings or revivals. Community and nurture are essential to historical Christianity, noticeably so in early Protestantism. But the spread of Christianity on the frontier by itinerant preachers through revivals undermined the balance that should exist between the individual's affirmation of the self, forming a personal relationship with Christ, and the individual's giving up the self in order to be subsumed into Christ and become part of the family of God. Attention was placed on gaining adherents and the moment and the experience of conversion, less on knowledge of essential Christian practices and beliefs and nurturing the new Christians into a life commensurate with the teachings of Jesus.

True community, learning about the traditions and heritage of the faith, and growing into a greater likeness of Christ are essential aspects of Christianity. In his introduction to the *Handbook*, the author indicates an intent in forthcoming chapters to focus on Christians' adoption of a radically new ethic and philosophy of life. Although individual commitment was required, both nurture and participation in a community of faith were also hallmarks of early Methodism.

A Road Map for What Follows

The introduction concludes by raising a few reflective questions and by providing a road map for the chapters that follow. Are we addressing the needs of God's people? What does it mean to be a Methodist or like-minded Protestant in the twenty-first century? Who are we called to be? And what are we called to do? Discovering our roots, the author affirms, will show Christians the way back to a more genuine church community. The past is a point of departure for our dialogue about our present-day faith.

As for the road map, outside of an introduction and conclusion, the *Handbook* (and the certification course on Spiritual and Church Renewal) is divided into five topics. *Topic I. Longing for God* concerns the human condition and also takes a closer look at God's commandments. *Topic II. The Door of Religion* examines the relationship between God and people, discusses grace or God's kindness, the Christian's faith and search for holiness, and the stream of pietism and religious devotion that so much influenced American Methodism and like-minded Protestants. *Topic III. How Do We Know the Truth about God, Ourselves, and Our Intended Relationship with the World?* looks at Protestant Christianity's approach to knowing truth—focusing on the Bible but also through studying history, being guided by reason, and appreciating sentiments. *Topic IV. Inclusion in the Family of God* is devoted to the Christian ideal of inclusiveness and its often sad betrayal in American Christianity. Chapters feature discussions about women's struggle for full participation in institutional Christianity; the racial division that has marred American Christianity; and the current division in Methodism over ordination and marriage of self-avowed, practicing LGBTQ+ church members. *Topic V. The Nature and Task of the Church* includes expositions concerning evangelism; Christian missions; Christian social ministries; and an examination of the nature and institutional structure of the church, church governance, and organization. And finally, in the conclusion, the *Handbook* draws together suggestions for the future of American Christianity—a church for today.

Terms, Dates, Events, and People

Define, identify, or explain each word or phrase as they appear in the *Handbook*'s introduction. Ask your instructor or look up words or phrases that remain unclear.

- agnostics

- atheists
- camp meetings
- Christian denominations
- Christian identity
- cultural religion
- evangelical wing of the Anglican Church
- Francis Asbury
- Gallup Poll
- God's people
- Methodists and like-minded Protestants
- "nones"
- Pentecostal preachers
- Pew Forum on Religion and Religious Life
- prophetic voice
- Public Religion Research Institute
- relationship with Christ
- religions as voluntary associations
- religious hypocrisy
- revivalism
- Second Great Awakening
- seekers

Reading Comprehension

Explain these important themes found in the *Handbook*'s introduction. Discuss them with course partners. If the *Handbook for the Christian Faith*'s author were in the room with you, what questions would you ask? Can you think of further evidence to buttress the points the author makes?

1. Statistical data shows that church membership and attendance have been steadily decreasing for thirty years.
2. Many self-identifying Christians demonstrate pervasive ignorance about essential practices and beliefs of their faith.

3. American Christianity is at a crossroads and faces a critical moment. Changes regarding the religious makeup of the United States and the status and influence of Christianity in America are already being strongly felt. Denial and typical reactionary responses will not alter the current trajectory. Neither will they expose the underlying causes of American Christianity's malaise.

4. However, the current crisis in American religion presents believers the opportunity to rediscover and reexamine their Christian roots. The decision that confronts Methodists and like-minded Protestants concerns how they will react to the challenge of the times.

5. While American Christianity includes essential practices and beliefs of the faith, it also includes aspects alien to historical Christianity. The task of self-examination is not easy. Besides effort, it requires us to be completely honest about ourselves and our churches.

6. Although there is hypocrisy and corruption in Christianity, a majority of Christians are well-meaning people of faith trying each day to live moral lives and wanting to be followers of Christ. They wish to know more about their faith and to grow into being better disciples of Christ. Criticism should not purpose to demean, embarrass, or shame opponents, but to persuade all to a better future.

7. The busyness of American life often hinders the amount of time Christians devote to learning about their faith and applying its teachings to daily living.

8. Busyness is not the only obstacle to learning more about the Christian faith and leading a life commensurate with its teachings. In America, religions are voluntary associations of like-minded people. And while many aspects of this voluntarism are positive, consequences include the sometimes-unhealthy mixing of religion and culture with the loss of Christianity's prophetic voice.

9. Nineteenth- and early twentieth-century revivalism spurred the rapid growth of evangelical Protestantism in America. Accompanying the growth, we find shift in emphases away from the Christian community toward the individual, also away from nurture in Christian living to the moment and experience of conversion.

10. The *Handbook for the Christian Faith* and the course on Spiritual and Church Renewal purpose to do more than lead to a better understanding of Christianity as a religion. Their goal also is to aid participants as they try to understand themselves as Christians. Dialogue with the

past should lead to better insight into the present and future. Doing theology is to bear witness. And reflecting on the current crisis in American religion in light of faith's writings and traditions may lead to truer Christianity, especially if followed by further reflection and action in continuous progress into a Christlike community and philosophy of living.

Exercises to Enhance Understanding

1. Learn the history of your local congregation. Interview the minister(s) and some of the older members. Is there a written history of your church? Are there written records? Old photographs? When was the church founded? Do the descendants of some of the founders still frequent services? How have Christians affected your community for the better?

2. Share the information you uncover with your discussion partners. Discuss ways that you can help the local congregation become more aware of its rich heritage.

3. Has your congregation experienced a decreasing membership? In your group, discuss reasons for the decrease. Are there actions that the congregation can take to reach out to the community? The concluding chapter to this book offers some concrete tried-and-true suggestions for revitalizing your congregation.

Suggested Readings

Jones, Jeffrey M. "U.S. Church Membership Falls Below Majority for First Time." *Gallup*, March 29, 2021. https://news.gallup.com/poll/341963/church-membership-fallsbelow-majority-first-time.aspx.

Mead, Sidney E. *The Lively Experiment: The Shaping of Christianity in America*. New York: Harper & Row, 1963.

Newport, Frank. "2017 Update on Americans and Religion." *Gallup*, December 22, 2017. https://gallup.com/poll/224642/2017-update-americans-religion-aspx.

Pew Research Center (PRC). "In U.S., Decline of Christianity Continues at Rapid Pace." PRC, October 17, 2019. https://www.pewresearch.org/religion/2019/10/17/in-u-s-decline-of-christianity-continues-at-rapid-pace/.

———. "U.S. Religious Knowledge Survey." PRC, September 28, 2010. https://www.pewforum.org/2010/09/28/u-s-religious-knowledge-survey/.

———. "What Americans Know about Religion." PRC, July 23, 2019. https://www.pewforum.org/2019/07/23/what-americans-know-about-religion/.

The PRRI Staff. "The 2020 Census of American Religion." Public Religions Research Institute (PRRI), July 8, 2021. https://www.prri.org/research/2020-census-of-american-religion/.

Richey, Russell E., et al. *American Methodism: A Compact History*. Nashville: Abingdon, 2010–12.

1

The Human Condition

Overview and Summary of Content

PART I OF THE *Handbook for the Christian Faith* opens with theology, specifically with a theological description of the human being. The first chapter emphasizes two bedrock Christian affirmations: 1) that people were created by God and thus carry his divine nature; while at the same time 2) they are fallen creatures who have separated themselves from God. The chapter recalls how Methodism is rooted in the Anglican community, emerging during the first third of the eighteenth century as a renewal movement among a small group of people led by two clergymen from the Church of England: the brothers John and Charles Wesley. These brothers were especially committed to living out their faith and did not seek to create new doctrine. Rather, they wished to tap into the essential beliefs of Christianity rooted in the gospel proclaimed by the early church.

The Human Desire to Be Near God

"For what end did God create man?" In keeping with the teachings of the Anglican catechism, Wesley answered, "To glorify and enjoy Him forever," but he went on to explain that God made all things, including people, to be happy—which comes through companionship with God. Christians believe that people long for God. Our place is with God and our lives are not right until we are with God. And God, too, delights when we are near.

Creatures display qualities of their creator. From the wellspring of Christianity comes the biblical description of people created in the image and likeness of God. And Christianity affirms that people long to be like their creator, connected with their own true nature. What does it mean to be near God? Methodists and like-minded Christians affirm that humans were created with the abilities to love, show mercy, kindness, desire justice, think rationally, enjoy work, etc.; and also to grow in holiness, develop in wisdom and understanding, see patterns of cause and effect, care for the earth, become cocreators with God, artisans of a better society. People are near to God when they are praising and thanking him. And they are happiest and feel most fulfilled when they are acting and thinking in accordance to their nature as creations of God.

Sin and Separation from God

But Christianity also affirms that human nature became corrupted. And because the inclination to evil separates us from God, we need to repent—that is to change our heart and way of being in the world. The call to repentance goes back to Jesus' earliest proclamation and recaptures also a main emphasis of the Hebrew prophets.

Although commonplace in the history of Christianity and at the time Methodism established itself, both the language and the concept of sin have for the most part vanished from consciousness today. They have been replaced in part by laws and notions of criminality, in part by the medical language and our understanding of the symptoms of mental disorders and diseases, and in part by a view of collective actions where individual responsibility evaporates. But there are consequences when individuals and society no longer assume responsibility for what used to be considered sin. So, it is important to recapture for the twenty-first century the original meaning of the Christian notion of sin. Basically, the biblical language expresses three groups of meanings.

Sin as Collateral Damage

The most common meaning of the numerous words from the Hebrew Old Testament and Greek New Testament that are translated "sin" in English versions of the Bible is simply "missing the mark." The *Handbook* fastens on to the phrase "collateral damage," picking up on the idea of an action that causes unintended harm. Many times, such sins arise from inaction, oversight, frustrations, or other mindless behavior. But whether through action or inaction, purposeful or not, people bear responsibility for those decisions that cause harm.

Sin as Consequences of Rebellion

Several Hebrew and Greek terms that are translated "sin" in the Bible fit more with the concept of the consequences of rebellion or willful disobedience. Emphasis is placed on the voluntary, conscious nature of the actions—thus, how the actions show rebellion against God and against our own human nature as created in the image and likeness of God. John Wesley himself preferred to reserve the English word sin for this usage, using the words "offenses" and "transgressions" for the involuntary breaking of divine law that accompanies ignorance or arises from error. As with missing the mark, human choice plays its part, but the choice betrays volition to sin. Sins can be of commission or omission. People know that what they are contemplating will bring about harm but continue with their plans. The sin is premeditated.

The *Handbook*'s author points out that people's desire to follow their own course, even when reason, conscience, personal experience, and wisdom passed down from others tells them that to do so will bring catastrophic harm, is so strong that it appears as a force of its own. Mysteriously, this force seems part of our human nature yet also seems apart from it. Furthermore, religious people brought up in the church should be much more aware of what God demands than are others who must glean what can be known about God solely from observing his power and his creation. For Christians, their sin is more clearly rebellion. It is pride, the rebellion of loving ourselves over God and God's creation, selecting to think and act our way instead of as God commanded. And finally, while Christians might well control certain actions, people's sinful nature is betrayed by their thoughts.

Sin as Both the Cause and Consequence of Separation from God

A third group of terms in the Bible define sin as the cause and consequence of our separation from God. Such can distort people's nature as the separation also causes distancing from those qualities of God imbued in people through creation. The author adds that separation occurs not because God wills it but results from human free choice.

Where Do We Go from Here?

The author concludes the chapter by reminding his readers (and the participants in the Spiritual and Church Renewal course) that Methodists and the like-minded emphasize Christian living. By incorporating greater spirituality into their lives, Christians will enjoy more happiness and inner peace. And the greater spirituality of the believer will also affect others in a positive manner, bringing greater justice and love to them and society as a whole.

As practical advice, the author recommends that Christians work at reconnecting with themselves as they were created to be. They should reconsider their interior life, examining habits of private prayers, meditations, reflections, and time spent on task. Being closer to God requires commitment, time, and a willing heart. And in step with the organized, methodical approach of Methodism, the author sketches out a daily plan of beginning each day spending time with God in prayer and meditation, returning periodically to converse with God during the day, and ending each day's activities in prayer.

What should our prayers be like? All prayers should start and end with thanksgiving. People should ask for forgiveness for acts that they have wittingly or unwittingly done to bring harm to God's creation. The habit of prayer should include the sharing of needs. And the prayers should always ask God to show ways to be of service to him. An important part of prayer is learning to listen to what God says.

Terms, Dates, Events, and People

Define, identify, or explain each word and phrase as they appear in the *Handbook*'s chapter 1. Ask your instructor or look up words or phrases that remain unclear.

- Anglican Society for the Propagation of the Gospel
- catechism
- Charles Wesley
- Christian philosophy of living
- Church of England
- created in the image of God
- created in the likeness of God
- fifteen-five-five commitment
- Groupthink
- habit of prayer
- the human condition
- inclination to evil

- John Wesley (1703–91)
- ordained
- prayer as listening
- reconnecting with ourselves as creations of God
- sin
- sin as the cause and consequence of separation from God
- sin as consequence of rebellion
- sin as missing the mark or as collateral damage
- theological compendium
- the Thirty-nine Articles of Religion

Reading Comprehension

Explain these important themes found in chapter 1. Discuss them with course partners. If the *Handbook for the Christian Faith*'s author were in the room with you, what questions would you ask? Can you think of further evidence to buttress the points the author makes?

1. American Methodism (and like-minded Christianity) developed from the Church of England. The essential doctrines of this branch of Christianity are rooted in earliest Christianity.

2. The Anglican clerics John and Charles Wesley are considered the founders of Methodism. They visited America in 1735, setting the course and deeply influencing this branch of American religion.

3. Humans were created by God, in his image and likeness. Thus, human nature is imbued with characteristics of God, like an understanding and capability for justice, mercy, and love, and the ability to progress in understanding the world around us and to structure society more in keeping with God's will.

4. Being God's creations, humans long for companionship with God and are not fully at peace with themselves and the world around them when separated from their creator. And God, too, wishes for a close relationship with people.

5. While being created good and having a nature commensurate with their creator, people also betray an inclination to evil. This powerful inclination betrays the intended and natural character of people as

created in the image and likeness of God and leads people away from doing justice, mercy, love, etc.

6. The language and concept of sin have largely disappeared in America, displaced by laws and notions of criminality, medical language and a modern understanding of the symptoms of mental disorders and diseases, and a view of collective actions where individual responsibility evaporates.

7. In order to understand the essential beliefs and practices of Christianity, twenty-first-century Methodists and like-minded American Christians must recapture the old notions of sin. While numerous Hebrew and Greek words are translated as "sin," basically there are three biblical notions of sin: sin as missing the mark, sin as rebellion, and sin as separation.

8. Sin as missing the mark or as collateral damage commonly occurs when someone through inaction, oversight, frustrations, or other mindless behavior makes a decision that causes harm. Whether through action or inaction, purposeful or not, the person bears responsibility for the hurtful consequences of that decision.

9. Sin as consequences of rebellion emphasizes the voluntary, conscious nature of actions that arise from the person's distorted self-reliance. The actions show rebellion against God and against that person's own nature as created in God's image and likeness. The person is aware that harm will occur and continues with the decision anyway. The sin is premeditated.

10. Sin as the cause and consequence of separation from God results from distancing oneself from God and those qualities of the divine that became part of human nature through creation. Such separation distorts us and our perception of reality.

11. Connecting more closely with God means reconnecting with ourselves as we were created to be. First steps include examining and changing habits of private prayers, meditations, and reflections. Being closer to God requires commitment, time, and a willing heart. Christians can develop the custom of conversing with God. Listening to God is an important part of prayer.

Exercises to Enhance Understanding

1. Repeat the following prayer of confession: "Almighty God, Father of our Lord Jesus Christ, maker of all things, judge of all people: We acknowledge and bewail our manifold sins and wickedness, which we from time to time most grievously have committed by thought, word, and deed, against thy divine majesty. We do earnestly repent and are heartily sorry for these our misdoings; the remembrance of them is grievous unto us. Have mercy upon us, most merciful Father. For thy Son our Lord Jesus Christ's sake, forgive us all that is past; and grant that we may ever hereafter serve and please thee in newness of life, to the honor and glory of thy name; through Jesus Christ our Lord, Amen."

2. This prayer makes part of a liturgy of Holy Communion (The United Methodist Church. "A Service of Word and Table IV." In *The United Methodist Hymnal: Book of United Methodist Worship*, 26–31. Nashville: The United Methodist Publishing House, 1987.). With your discussion group, share your thoughts concerning the meaning of the prayer in that context. How important is it to repent of sins before partaking of the Sacrament of the Lord's Supper?

3. The prayer closes with a petition for God's mercy. With partners in the course, discuss how good people who lead moral lives nevertheless need to ask daily for forgiveness.

Suggested Readings

From the Bible: Paul's Epistle to the Romans.

Burtner, Robert W., and Robert Chiles, eds. "Man." Chapter V in *A Compend of Wesley's Theology*, 107–36. Nashville: Abingdon, 1954.

The Church of England. "Articles of Religion." In *The Common Book of Prayer* (2022). https://www.churchofengland.org/prayer-and-worship/worship-texts-andresources/book-common-prayer/articles-religion.

Menninger, Karl. *Whatever Became of Sin?* New York: Hawthorn, 1973.

Niebuhr, Reinhold. *The Nature and Destiny of Man: A Christian Interpretation*. 2 vols. Louisville: Westminster-John Knox, 1996.

The United Methodist Church (UMC). "The Articles of Religion of the Methodist Church." 2016. http://www.umc.org/what-we-believe/the-articles-of-religion-of-the-methodist-church.

Williams, Colin W. *John Wesley's Theology Today: A Study of the Wesleyan Tradition in the Light of Current Theological Dialogue*, 47–56. Nashville: Abingdon, 1960.

2

Understanding God's Commandments

Overview and Summary of Content

CHAPTER 1 OF THE *Handbook for the Christian Faith* indicated that Methodism and Christianity in general are infinitely more concerned with sinners than with sin. But that is not always apparent in our American culture, where some adherents and many on the fringe of Christianity mischaracterize faith primarily as a set of dos and don'ts. In chapter 2, then, the author takes on the legalism associated with American religion. Jesus explained that the greatest commandments were to love God and to love the neighbor. On these two commandments hang all the law and the prophets (Matt 22:37–40; Mark 12:29–31; Luke 10:27; see Deut 6:5; Lev 18:18). Jesus also taught, "In everything do to others as you would have them do to you; for this is the law and the prophets" (Matt 7:12; cf. Luke 6:31). Besides locating some of the Bible's best-known laws in their historical-social context, the author emphasizes how Christianity's interpretation of the commandments is significantly more comprehensive than what popular culture assumes.

The Ten Commandments

Jewish tradition holds that there are 613 commandments in the Bible, many more than can be examined in a chapter in a handbook. So, the author concentrates attention on some laws that feature in American Christianity. He begins with the Ten Commandments as listed in Exodus 20:

1. I am the Lord your God, who brought you out of the land of Egypt, out of the house of slavery; . . . you shall have no other gods before me;
2. You shall not make for yourself an idol;
3. You shall not make wrongful use of the name of the Lord your God;

4. Remember the sabbath day and keep it holy;
5. Honor your father and your mother;
6. You shall not murder;
7. You shall not commit adultery;
8. You shall not steal;
9. You shall not bear false witness; and
10. You shall not covet . . . anything that belongs to your neighbor.

Surprisingly, not all denominations agree on the commandments to be included among the ten or their numbering.

The first four commandments concern honoring and reverencing God. The first checks the glorification of jobs, nation, groups, and sport teams, and calls into question the folly of relying on the gods that humans create. The second indicates much more than opposition to pagan deities or figurines of such deities, pointing out that mediation to God occurs through Jesus. Idols represent the work of human hands, and to worship idols is to worship ourselves. The third signifies the misappropriation of God's authority for our own purposes. The fourth is a reminder to separate enough from daily activities to be grateful to God. And followers of Jesus also know well that "the sabbath was made for humankind, not humankind for the sabbath" (Mark 2:27). Christians cannot escape the difficult task of weighing activities: "Is it lawful to do good or to do harm on the sabbath, to save life or to kill?" (Mark 3:1–5).

The closing six commandments concern relationships with other people. The fifth commandment expresses the importance to God of our family relations. And the author reminds us that Jesus expanded the concept of family. The sixth commandment is a reminder that life is precious to God and all Christians should see it as so. Jesus not only instructed his followers to keep the seventh commandment not to commit adultery but added that "anyone who looks at a woman lustfully has already committed adultery with her in his heart" (Matt 5:27–30). The *Handbook*'s author reminds us that in the United States approximately 50 percent of all marriages suffer the consequences of one of the spouses being unfaithful. The eighth commandment expands the concept of stealing much beyond modern American's criminal code, and Jesus himself broadened the meaning of the ninth commandment far beyond the justice system. Christianity stresses the importance of not using false or misleading speech. People should seek the truth and leave falsehoods behind. The tenth commandment, not to covet, goes beyond activities to motives. John Wesley held that Christians should live frugally and share what they had with others. He wished that all would give as much of their earnings as possible back to God's work.

The Seven Deadly Sins

Next, the *Handbook*'s author lists and discusses the groups of deadly or cardinal sins that Pope Gregory the Great and other Christians first grouped together during the early Middle Ages: pride, envy, wrath, acedia, avarice, gluttony, and lust. These represented attitudes and habits that proved especially destructive.

Pride is a sin when it becomes conceit, when people don't see themselves in their proper relationship to God and God's creation. When pride becomes self-deification, it is sin. Pride is a sin when self-love takes precedence over love of the neighbor and love of God. Envy is the desire for an attribute or possession that belongs to someone else. It indicates self-centeredness and lack of love for others. Wrath signifies an anger that leads to violent punishment for the perceived offender. While expressions of anger are justified on some occasions, for instance on behalf of others who are suffering injustices, the loss of control leading to violence and retribution is never justified. Acedia is more than simple laziness. It is a state of not caring about God's purposes, God's creation, the neighbor, and ultimately oneself. It leads to the inability to work, to do good, to be kind, to act with mercy. The sinner is disinterested in justice and heartless toward those who suffer. Avarice is an out-of-control self-centered desire to accumulate goods and wealth. Saint Augustine and other early Christians held that while both poor and rich were welcomed in the church, God demanded of the rich that they share with the poor what was superfluous to them but necessities for the poor. Christians are marked by generosity and equality (Jas 1:9–17; 2:1–8). The deep sin of gluttony is self-love through excess. It is at first the choice to seek pleasure above other considerations. And lust dehumanizes the other, transforming people into sexual objects; furthermore, when directed at intimacy outside of marriage, lust betrays the trust of partners and undermines the love that should reign between partners.

Other Individual Sins

The *Handbook*'s author continues explicating the deeper meaning of some of the Bible's precepts by discussing how blaspheming against the Holy Spirit is tantamount to consciously cutting oneself off from the life force that comes from God; how lying, duplicity, misrepresentation, and cheating destroy trust and sabotage love; how cruelty of all kinds, although present among us, are despicable to God; and how people are tasked by God to be caretakers of the world. Regarding this last point, the author reminds us that the earth and its natural resources were intended for all of creation. And this includes our and future generations. People are called to be proactive in protecting the environment.

Structural Sins

Although the discussion of individual sins in the *Handbook*'s chapter 2 is in keeping with the roots of Methodism's (and American Protestantism's) eighteenth- and nineteenth-century thinking about sin, the author points out that American religion has also spoken forcefully about structural sins. By structural sins, the author is referring to injustices borne from the way society is organized—from its laws, traditions in government, aspirations, morals, practices. An example of structural sin from our American past is slavery, an evil that permeated society and was codified into law.

There are bitter historical examples of structural sins in every chapter of history, and although not named as such, structural sins have always been clearly recognized by Christians. Conquering such sins entails changing the laws and structures of society. But the subject is complicated, and except for pointing out that not only the goal of a more just society but the means for change must comport with the teachings of Jesus, the author postpones further discussion on the topic until chapter 14 of the *Handbook*. The topic of that chapter is the Christian's call to do good individually and as members of society.

Where Do We Go from Here?

The author concludes the chapter with the reminder that prayer (or conversing with God) entails not only sharing our thoughts with God but listening to him. Reading the Bible is an important activity for Christians. The believer's and the church's current exchange with God fits within a dialogue that goes back to the days of Abraham four thousand years ago. Developing the habit of reading the Bible helps people develop a truer awareness of right and wrong. It is important to read Scripture for its content, that is to know exactly what is written. But it is even more important to discern the spirit or intent of God's commandments. The habit of reading the Bible should be accompanied by study and reflection on the purposes of God's word.

Terms, Dates, Events, and People

Define, identify, or explain each word and phrase as they appear in the *Handbook*'s chapter 2. Ask your instructor or look up words or phrases that remain unclear.

- Saint Anthony
- Augustine of Hippo
- Gregory the Great
- John Calvin and Calvinism
- John Knox
- just war doctrine
- Justin Martyr
- Levite
- Leviticus Holiness Code
- Liturgy of Hours
- Martin Luther
- *mincha*
- Origen
- philosophers and Stoic school of philosophy
- *pneuma*
- Reformed Tradition
- *ruach*
- Sabbath
- Samaritan
- seven deadly sins
- The *Shema*
- social justice
- structural sin
- United States Conference of Catholic Bishops

Reading Comprehension

Explain these important themes found in chapter 2. Discuss them with course partners. If the *Handbook for the Christian Faith*'s author were in the room with you, what questions would you ask? Can you think of further evidence to buttress the points the author makes?

1. Being a Christian is not as simple as following a set of rules, and keeping the commandments is more complicated than often thought. Jesus set a hierarchy to the Old Testament precepts. Loving God and loving the neighbor are of primary importance. Moreover, Jesus and the Scriptures themselves often broadened the meaning of the commandments. Thus, Christianity interprets the commandments more comprehensively than their caricature in popular culture allows.

2. Jesus also pointed out that knowing the commandments does not free Christians from decisions, especially from the difficult task of weighing good and harm. For instance, when keeping the precept not to work on the Sabbath, what is the better choice, to heal the man with the withered hand or not to heal him? (cf. Matt 12:9–14; Mark 3:1–6; Luke 6:6–11).

3. In keeping with Jesus' emphases, the Ten Commandments include several precepts about honoring God and several about loving the neighbor. But neither list is comprehensive.

4. Many of the ordinances in the Old Testament and some in the New Testament were culturally conditioned—ceremonial and civic laws and taboos that might have been appropriate for the time and place when first written but which might not be relevant today. At the same time, there is a deeper meaning embedded in many of the old laws that remains applicable to any age and culture. For example, the commandment to remember the Sabbath day and keep it holy reminds Christians to separate themselves from daily activities enough to be grateful to God. Study, discernment, and interpretation must accompany appropriation of the laws for the twenty-first century.

5. Besides actions, God's commandments concern inner thoughts, desires, and motives. There are many attitudes and habits not covered by our modern criminal codes or classification of symptoms of mental and physical disorders that nevertheless cause harm to oneself, others, and God's creation in general. The so-called seven deadly sins are of this type. Pride is harmful when it is self-love that takes precedence over love of the neighbor and love of God. While in some instances

expressions of anger are justified, the loss of control leading to violence and retribution is not justified. Christianity struggles to coexist with a materialism that places emphasis on the selfish accumulation of goods. Lies sabotage love by destroying trust and obscuring the intended nature of creation.

6. People can cut themselves off from the life-force that comes from God. When this takes place, it is not because God wills our separation from him. Rather, the separation occurs because of our decisions and because God granted us free will.

7. Christianity is not only concerned with individual sins like pride and envy but with structural sins. In brief, these are injustices borne from the way society is organized—from its laws, traditions in government, aspirations, morals, and practices. An example from America's past is slavery. Concerning present-day America, Christians should hold close their responsibility to be caretakers of God's planet and all living things on it.

8. Reading the Bible situates the church and individual Christians within a dialogue that goes back to the days of Abraham. Christians should both know the content and discern the spirit of the Bible's commandments. The habit of reading the Bible should be accompanied by historical study and also by reflection concerning the meaning of God's word for today.

Exercises to Enhance Understanding

1. How many of the Ten Commandments can you list from memory? Work in pairs or in small groups to see how many each person can remember correctly. Which commandments do most of us tend to remember?

2. Discuss the implications of displaying the Ten Commandments in public or government spaces. Is it more appropriate to display the commandments at courthouses or in churches? Are there places or spaces in your community where the Ten Commandments are displayed? What message does this send?

3. Consider the list and the author's discussion of the seven deadly sins. Which of these sins seem most serious or dangerous? Which do we

most ignore or overlook? Read Galatians 5:22–23. How might Paul's discussion of the fruits of the spirit counteract the seven deadly sins?

4. What is the difference between individual sins and structural sins? What are some examples of structural sin in the world or in your own community? In what ways are such structural sins connected to your own individual sin?

Suggested Readings

Augustine. *On Lying*. Translated by H. Browne. Nicene and Post-Nicene Fathers. First series, 3. Edited by Philip Schaff. Buffalo, NY: Christian Literature, 1888. New Advent. Revised and edited for New Advent by Kevin Knight. https://www.newadvent.org/fathers/1312.

Cahill, Thomas. *The Gifts of the Jews: How a Tribe of Desert Nomads Changed the Way Everyone Thinks and Feels*. New York: Doubleday, 1998.

Friedberg, Albert D. *Crafting the 613 Commandments: Maimonides on the Enumeration, Classification, and Formation of the Spiritual Commandments*. Boston: Academic Studies, 2013.

Hayes, John H. *Interpreting Israelite History, Prophecy, and Law*. Edited and introduced by Brad E. Kelle. Eugene, OR: Cascade, 2013.

Jamison, Carol. "The New Seven Deadly Sins." In *Defining Medievalism(s) II*, edited by Karl Fugelso, 2:265–87. Studies in Medievalism 18. Woodbridge, UK: Boydell & Brewer, 2009.

Luther, Martin. *Commentary on the Sermon on the Mount*. Translated by Charles A. Hay. Bellingham, WA: Lexham, 2017.

3

Repentance and Grace

Overview and Summary of Content

PART II OF THE *Handbook for the Christian Faith* addresses beliefs that Methodists and like-minded Christians hold essential. Chapter 3 opens by recounting an emotion-laden, going-to-the altar experience common among adolescent evangelicals. Although conversion experiences mark the lives of some Christians, the author points out that the momentary feeling that accompanies such an event is not nearly as meaningful as the path into a new life that should follow. A relationship with God is a daily walk and a lifelong journey.

Repentance

Christianity's understanding of repentance is significantly deeper than the caricature of it. Repentance entails embarking on a new life, which for the purposes of analysis can be thought of as consisting of three parts: contrition, confession, and an earnest deposit on the new life.

Contrition is a new state of being that includes the feeling of sadness and the sense of remorse for actions and thoughts out-of-step with God's expectations. It is the internal acknowledgement that our sins have been harmful to God, other people, and God's creation. Contrition is not just a statement of being sorry, but it is the true feeling of regret and sorrow.

From an early age, most people experience feeling guilt. At such moments they find that they have performed acts or had thoughts unacceptable to their own deeper values. There is an internal realization that they are not who they think they should be. Where does the guilt come from? Christianity holds that by being created in the image and likeness of God people were created with a consciousness of right and wrong.

But it is complicated, for Christianity also affirms that sin has so corrupted human nature that people cannot fully trust their innate sense of right and wrong or even their feelings of guilt. Since guilt is not only a natural human feeling but is also learned behavior, it can be distorted. People can become so callous as to feel no guilt, they can learn to feel guilty about the wrong things, and they can hide their guilt from themselves and others. So, feelings of guilt and remorse are not fully trustworthy. And more importantly, even when legitimate, private feelings in themselves aren't sufficient to make up for the real damage done to others and God's creation. Repairing a wronged relationship calls for not only inward change but outward action.

So, in Christianity reconciliation calls for the confession of sin. While Roman Catholics require an oral confession before a priest as a step in their Sacrament of Penance and Reconciliation, Protestants hold that there is only one mediator, Christ. Should Christians confess their sins directly to those aggrieved? Sometimes it is possible and appropriate to seek out those harmed and to express feelings of sadness and remorse directly to them; sometimes not. But always, Christians must confess their sins before God for having offended him and his creation.

But even when paired with contrition, confession cannot return individuals and society to the healthier condition that preceded sin. The third part of repentance, the earnest deposit, equates to the first steps taken toward a new life. Such steps are symbolic and show intention. Do these first steps, then, bring about repentance? Methodists and like-minded Christians hold that ultimately not. Try as people may, it is beyond human effort to right wrongs completely. Industry and human will alone cannot reconcile people to God and his creation. Humans need help.

Preceding Grace

If people's best efforts are not enough to put right the wrongs they have committed and knit together broken relationships with others and God, how does repentance occur? Following Paul, Augustine, Luther, Zwingli, Calvin, and Wesley, almost all Protestants confess that people are justified not through their own actions but through the grace of Christ. What does that mean? Grace is goodwill or favor, and the grace of Christ is a shorthand way of referring to the undeserved favor from God that comes to people through the life, ministry, and passion of Jesus. This goodwill is always surrounding people, encouraging them, and wishing to help. But one of God's gifts to humans was free will, our ability to accept or not accept God's favor. There is a great mystery surrounding the transformation that occurs in repentance, but people should not underestimate the work of the Holy Spirit in preparing them for change. God's love disposes people for change. Preceding grace is that divine grace that operates on people's will before they turn to God, preparing them for change.

Justifying Grace

It is a tenet of Christianity that people are justified—that is, placed in a right relationship with God—and delivered from sin and death through God's grace in Christ. As it was when God created Adam out of the dust of the earth and breathed his breath into him, bestowing unto humans the gift of life, so salvation (or ultimate well-being) is likewise unearned. It is a gift from a merciful God who loves his creation. And if people, with God's help, trust in this God as revealed in the life, teachings, and passion of Christ, repent of sins, and subsume their will to his, salvation ensues. At that point, they can become so different as to be a new creation. The human part is to trust in that gift from God and be subsumed into his will.

Election?

Being justified by God and not by human actions can seem near incomprehensible to those holding to God's justice, goodness, and mercy. Why do some seem so favored by God and others not? The *Handbook*'s author points out that for believers, salvation always seems unmerited. God's love is a gift that comes to sinners as unexpected grace. And for every person who has experienced such moments of wonder, there is always a sense of election. But that does not necessarily mean that the creator arbitrarily chose to favor some people and not others. Methodists and the like-minded hold rather that God intended the well-being made possible through Christ's life, teachings, and passion for all. As Father and Creator, God loves all his creation. But not all people accept God's love. Choice accompanies human independence. People have free will and some choose not to respond.

Justification by Faith

What is salvation like? The author examines several elements taken from John Wesley's sermon entitled "Salvation by Faith." It is a present salvation. People's actions and this world are important to God. It is salvation from original and actual past and present sin. This includes being delivered from guilt before God from our past sins. It is salvation from fear of the wrath of God. Where people once experienced fear, now there is peace. It is salvation from the power of sin, so people can progress in holiness. And it is salvation from habitual sin. And in other sermons, Wesley pointed out that salvation is not only deliverance *from* but is also freedom or empowerment *to*. People are saved in order to lead holy lives, to seek justice, and to spread the good news of Christ and to join him in announcing that God's kingdom is at hand. In sum, being justified by God means to take on God's purposes for oneself.

Where Do We Go from Here?

Who are Christians called to be? And what are they called to do? The *Handbook*'s author suggests that Christians must go beyond the solitary tasks mentioned in earlier chapters of praying, reading the Bible, and meditating. As Jesus' disciples did not remain on the mountainside in private prayer, twenty-first-century Christians should take steps toward a new life. They should surround themselves with others to receive and share love. On the path to becoming new creations, followers of Christ need encouragement and correction. Forming a discipleship group can facilitate God's work. The author suggests a group with voluntary membership, as with the first disciples small enough to allow bonding and strong personal relationships. The one requirement for joining would be that all in the group must be singularly committed to walking more closely with our Lord. The group would meet periodically, at set times, in an orderly fashion. The author suggests a leader or convener for the group who is not a member of the church's clergy. The group should be characterized by kindness, encouragement, honesty, correction, and love.

Terms, Dates, Events, and People

Define, identify, or explain each word and phrase as they appear in the *Handbook*'s chapter 3. Ask your instructor or look up words or phrases that remain unclear.

- confession
- contrition
- earnest deposit
- the elect
- grace

- holiness
- justification by faith
- Karl Jaspers
- predestination
- prevenient or preceding grace
- repentance
- Sacrament of Penance and Reconciliation
- salvation
- William Holman Hunt

Reading Comprehension

Explain these important themes found in chapter 3. Discuss them with course partners. If the *Handbook for the Christian Faith*'s author were in the room with you, what questions would you ask? Can you think of further evidence to buttress the points the author makes?

1. A relationship with Christ does not rest on one event but is built on many moments. The religious life is a daily walk and a lifelong journey.

2. Repentance is more than simply feeling remorse. It entails admitting guilt and embarking on a new life. For repentance to take place, there must be contrition, confession, and an earnest deposit on a new life.

3. Although humans were created in the image and likeness of God with consciousness of right and wrong, sin has so corrupted human nature that we cannot fully trust our innate sense of right and wrong.

4. Methodists and like-minded Christians hold that contrition and confession of sins are not sufficient to repair the damage caused by sin. Neither punishments nor human suffering can right the wrongs. Even changed actions and dispositions cannot fully undo the harm caused by sins. Complete reconciliation with God, other people, and the world is not something that people can do on their own.

5. Grace is goodwill or favor, and the grace of Christ is a shorthand way of referring to the undeserved favor of God that comes to people through the life, ministry, passion, and resurrection of Jesus. Methodists and the like-minded affirm that God intended his grace for all, not

just some people. Christ lived, taught, suffered, died, and rose from the dead for all.

6. Methodists and like-minded Christians hold that God's love is always surrounding us, working with us. But one of God's gifts to humans was free will, our ability to accept or not accept God's love and favor. God's invitation is always open, but some people refuse to respond to God's love. And some people go even further and completely shut themselves off from God.

7. Justifying grace is the undeserved and unmerited well-being or salvation that comes from God. As it was when God created Adam from the dust of the earth and breathed his breath into him, bestowing to humans the gift of life, salvation also is an unmerited gift. It comes from a merciful God who loves and refuses to abandon his creation.

8. Aware of our own inability to mend what has been torn apart, God's grace strikes recipients as an unexplainable gift. "What have I done to deserve this? And why has God chosen to bless me when so many others seem more deserving?" are natural questions. Yes, God's grace is mysterious and his ways inscrutable.

9. When thinking of grace, Christians too often focus exclusively on what they are receiving. But being justified by God also means to take on God's purposes for our lives. What are we called to do? And who are we called to become?

10. The love of God surrounds us in surprising ways. But most often, God's love reaches us through the lives and influences of other people. Being surrounded by other people provides us the opportunity to receive their love and also to share our love with them.

Exercises to Enhance Understanding

1. Reflect on the author's statement that " a relationship with Christ does not rest on one event but is built on many moments." In what ways does this reflect your own religious or spiritual experience, if at all? In pairs or in groups, discuss what it means to be in relationship with Christ.

2. Have you had a personal conversion experience? In pairs or in small groups, share any stories of such experiences? What was the setting? What did you feel at that moment? How has this experience impacted

your understanding of faith and discipleship? In what ways did this experience change your life or perspective?

3. How does repentance occur or take place? How do you understand the great mystery of change or transformation that happens through repentance? If God's grace is offered freely to us, in what specific ways is repentance necessary?

Suggested Readings

Burtner, Robert W., and Robert Chiles, eds. "Salvation." Chapter VI in *A Compend of Wesley's Theology*, 137–92. Nashville: Abingdon, 1954.

James, William. *The Varieties of Religious Experience: A Study in Human Nature*. The Gifford Lectures on Natural Religion Delivered at Edinburgh, 1901–2. New York: The New American Library, 1958.

Otto, Rudolf. *The Idea of the Holy: An Inquiry into the Non-rational Factor in the Idea of the Divine and Its Relation to the Rational*. Translated by John W. Harvey. Oxford: Oxford University Press, 1958.

Outler, Albert C. *Theology in the Wesleyan Spirit*. Nashville: Tidings, 1975.

Stendahl, Krister. *Paul among Jews and Gentiles*, 23–39. Minneapolis: Fortress, 1976.

Williams, Colin W. *John Wesley's Theology Today: A Study of the Wesleyan Tradition in the Light of Current Theological Dialogue*, 39–44; 57–73. Nashville: Abingdon, 1960.

4

Conversion?

Overview and Summary of Content

THE *HANDBOOK*'S CHAPTER 4 opens with the question, "Is a conversion experience necessary? No. Methodism and American Protestantism appreciate born-again experiences but do not insist on them. And in general, American Protestantism has preferred the word "awakened" to the word conversion. What most characterizes salvation is letting go of the self and trusting in God. The event can be dramatic; or, it can be a quiet moment. And it is more correct to think of moments, plural, than moment, singular, in passing.

The Use of Analogy to Describe Justification by Faith

What happens when being justified by faith? Theologians and ministers often describe salvation as a leap of faith—as when the trapeze artist at the circus lets go of her hold and somersaults through the air to be caught securely by her partner swinging on another trapeze. The image of a leap emphasizes the trust involved. It is a moment of complete dependence on God. Also helpful is the analogy of new insight. At some point in life, most people have experienced a *eureka* or aha! moment, and believers often describe their religious experiences as new sight or new understanding. However described, the justifying grace of God brings the assurance of God's love. And it brings a new state of being, a new prioritizing of what is and is not important.

Models of Faith

Different perspectives provide insights into faith. The book of Hebrews of the Bible was written at a time of persecution when many Christians were drifting away from their faith. For that community, the writer of Hebrews described faith as "the assurance of things hoped for, the conviction of things not seen" and encouraged his fellow Christians by pointing to the faith of Old Testament personages (see Heb 11:1—12:12). The writer closed his exhortation by urging Christians to "run with perseverance the race that is set before us, looking to Jesus the pioneer and perfecter of our faith" (Heb 12:1–2).

The *Handbook*'s author asks what are some other models of faith for twenty-first-century Methodists and like-minded Christians? And, then he sketches out how five widely known Christians experienced justification by faith.

Paul of Tarsus († 64)

The Apostle Paul who was traveling from Jerusalem to Syria to persecute Christians experienced a life-altering change when confronted by the Lord. Paul himself became a Christian, was filled with the Holy Spirit, and saw himself called to become an apostle to the nations (Acts 9:1–18). Later, as he reflected on the event, Paul understood how God's preceding grace had prepared him for his encounter. It seemed to him that God had always had a plan for him.

Was Paul's encounter a conversion or a calling experience? The *Handbook*'s author concludes that there are elements of both. What occurred was a conversion in the sense that Paul moved from an old perception of the law to a new understanding of freedom under the law; from an old expectation of the Messiah to a new vision of the Christ; and from an old dread of an advancing Christianity to a keen awareness that he himself was called to proclaim the gospel. He stopped persecuting Christians, but he didn't stop considering himself a Jew. Most telling, Paul's awakening signified a movement away from the self toward Christ. What occurred was a calling experience in that Paul took on a new mission. Instead of seeking out and persecuting Christians, Paul saw himself called by God to become an apostle to the nations.

Augustine of Hippo (354–430)

Saint Augustine of Hippo's description of becoming a Christian in the *Confessions* shows an interior struggle to overcome desire. The struggle joins aspects of both a long process and of a sudden event. After years of trying different philosophies and also experiencing the good influence of other

Christians, the struggle came to a head when in his late thirties Augustine felt directed by God to read a passage in Paul's letter to the Romans. "Let us live honorably as in the day, not in reveling and drunkenness, not in debauchery and licentiousness, not in quarreling and jealousy. Instead, put on the Lord Jesus Christ, and make no provision for the flesh, to gratify its desires" (Rom 13:13–14). As he finished reading, as if instantly, he felt secure with all doubt vanishing away. But Augustine's awakening, if we may call it that, continued past that singular event of insight into the future. For his plan had been to retire along with a few companions to the contemplative life of prayer, study, and meditation. Instead, he found himself pulled into the active life of Bishop of Hippo, dealing with a multitude of practical problems. He became one of the most important church leaders in history, setting the course for Christianity throughout the Middle Ages.

The *Handbook*'s author explores some of the similarities and differences between Augustine's and Paul's religious experiences. The differences are significant. But, there is great commonality with their realization of being justified by faith and not by their own efforts. Both men placed their futures in God's hands. Their newfound trust in God led both to take a radically new direction in life.

Martin Luther (1483–1546)

The great Reformer's religious experience is overlaid with legend. Raised in a strict Christian household and holding to an image of God as a harsh, unforgiving father, Luther left his studies in law to become an Augustinian monk. And it was only after being ordained a priest that Luther enjoyed what would be his formative religious experience. Urged by the vicar John von Staupitz and fellow friars to discover the joy and liberation brought by the gospel and given the responsibility to teach a course on Paul's writings, Luther came to understand the deeper meaning of Paul's statement "the just shall live by faith" (Rom 1:17). Luther did not need to earn his heavenly Father's love. Rather, Luther could trust that God's love as seen in the coming of Christ was freely given. This insight of salvation by faith, only by faith, was Luther's true conversion.

Again, we see a process. Luther's realization occurred four years after first entering the monastery. For those years and many before, God's preceding grace had been laying the groundwork for Luther's insight into God's love. And afterwards? God used Luther's remarkable talents to lead the northern European protest against the sale of indulgences, the trust in relics, simony, and corruptions of many kinds in the church; as he translated the Bible into German and argued to make the Scriptures available to every man; and as, in general, he became a rallying figure for renewing the church.

John Wesley (1703–91)

Wesley was the son and grandson of clerics, raised in a household of faith. He studied at Oxford, was ordained a deacon, and later a priest. He served as a minister and a missionary. And yet, it was only when he was thirty-five that Wesley had the experience that so marked his life. Before then, he doubted his own faith, felt himself depressed over real and imagined failings, and did not think he was making much headway in his life.

The experience occurred during a mid-week evening worship meeting at Aldersgate Street Chapel when Wesley heard an unnamed layperson read Luther's "Preface to the Epistle to the Romans." He felt his heart strangely warmed and received an inner assurance that Christ had removed his sins and that he could unfailingly trust in Christ.

The *Handbook*'s author parallels the sudden arrival of Wesley's assurance of salvation with the long preparation. In Wesley's view, the preparatory grace of God had long been active before he was justified by faith. God's preceding grace helped open Wesley to the possibilities of that heart-warming moment. And again, as with the models of Paul, Augustine, and Luther, the author references the changed life that follows and hints at the changed mission in life that would mark American religion.

Mother Teresa of Calcutta (1910–97)

The final model of faith explored in the *Handbook*'s chapter 4 is Mother Teresa, born in what today is the Republic of North Macedonia, but who is most famous for her work in India and other parts of the world. After detailing Mother Teresa's childhood experience of religion and her decision at eighteen to become a missionary by joining the Sisters of Loreto, the author points to her so-called "call within a call" during her mid-thirties to devote herself to caring for the poor, the sick, and the dying and how that progressed into the founding of the Missionaries of Charity that today minister to the hungry, the blind, lepers, and people who feel unwanted throughout the world. Again, we have the model of the conversion experience that at the same time has elements of a calling experience. Although a realization takes place suddenly, in retrospect, the long preparation is also evident. And the experience is not completed with the new insight that emerges. Rather, the experience ripples out into the world.

Where Do We Go from Here?

Religious language is metaphor and analogy. And the *Handbook*'s author holds that we can learn about God's grace and about the experience of religion by looking at Christians who have modeled faith in their lives. He offers an adage: "You become the company you keep" and proposes that we surround ourselves with Christian models of faith from whom to learn and emulate—the first being Jesus, the pioneer and perfecter of our faith (Heb 12:2). And the author proposes, too, that we can model a Christian philosophy of living for others. Let's remember our responsibility as models of faith, he urges, and the mysterious consequences for good that God engenders.

Terms, Dates, Events, and People

Define, identify, or explain each word and phrase as they appear in the *Handbook*'s chapter 4. Ask your instructor or look up words or phrases that remain unclear.

- atonement for sin
- awakenings, Great Awakening
- born-again
- a call and calling
- a call within the call
- Christian pilgrimage
- conversion
- Damascus Road experience
- *eidon*
- experience of call
- finding rest in God
- God as Father and judge
- hell
- indulgences
- John Wesley's Aldersgate experience
- kingdom of God
- movement away from the self toward Christ

- Paul of Tarsus
- pleasures of the flesh
- religious experiences
- religious language as metaphor and analogy
- *sola fide* or salvation by faith alone
- Saint Stephen
- Teresa of Calcutta

Reading Comprehension

Explain these important themes found in chapter 4. Discuss them with course partners. If the *Handbook for the Christian Faith*'s author were in the room with you, what questions would you ask? Can you think of further evidence to buttress the points the author makes?

1. Methodism appreciates born-again experiences but has not insisted on them. Methodism and American Protestantism in general have preferred the word "awakening" to "conversion."

2. Justification by faith is most often described through analogy. Common descriptors are "a leap of faith," which focuses on the trust and dependence on God, and "sudden new insight," which focuses on the new understanding of something that before seemed incomprehensible.

3. The justifying grace of God brings the assurance of God's love and salvation. And it brings a new state of being, a new prioritizing of what is and is not important.

4. Examining the lives of notable Christians provides different perspectives on faith and gives greater insight into the justifying grace of God. Christians can reach a better understanding of their faith by looking at other Christians who have modeled faith.

5. The Letter to the Hebrews in the Bible refers to Jesus as "the pioneer and perfecter of faith" (Heb 12:1–2). Christian models of faith are the Apostle Paul; Augustine, Bishop of Hippo; the Protestant Reformer Martin Luther; the founder of Methodism, John Wesley; and the twentieth-century's founder of the Missionaries of Charity, Mother Teresa of Calcutta.

6. The experiences of these models show elements of religious conversion and elements of a religious calling. To a certain extent the old self disappeared; the changed life led to new work and a new purpose. And there was a sense of being tasked by God with a mission.

7. While attention often focuses on the sudden heart-warming experience or moment of insight, in retrospect each person described long preceding periods of struggle and preparation.

8. To each model, the awakening signified a movement away from the self toward Christ. There was the realization that what had occurred came from God and not their own efforts.

9. The lives of these models of faith took new direction after the awakening event. The new direction was often unexpected and unplanned. The Apostle Paul, Saint Augustine, and the other models who are mentioned in the *Handbook* entrusted themselves and their future work to God. They were in God's hands.

10. As Christians surround themselves with models of faith, they too are models for others. Christians carry the responsibility of knowing that others might be learning from and emulating them. Perhaps the most common way to learn about God is to observe his love, mercy, justice, and active presence in others, including ourselves.

Exercises to Enhance Understanding

1. Can you identify people who have served as models of faith for you? In what ways have you tried to shape your daily living to reflect what you have learned from such people? What are specific qualities or attributes exemplified by your models of faith that you try to emulate? To whom might you serve as a model of faith?

2. Discuss the story of John Wesley's Aldersgate experience. Is this a story you had heard before? In pairs or in small groups, consider what Wesley meant by having his "heart strangely warmed." If you yourself have ever experienced such a moment, in what ways do you think God's preparatory grace had been active in the period leading up to that moment? Was this a moment when you felt assured of your salvation?

3. Respond to the author's statement that "religious language is metaphor and analogy" that helps us describe another reality. What are some

examples of religious language as metaphor? In what ways does the use of metaphor enhance our understanding of the gospel or of salvation?

Suggested Readings

From the Bible: The Apostle Paul's Damascus Road Experience is recounted three times in the Book of Acts (Acts 9:1–22; 22:3–21; 26:2–29) and mentioned by Paul himself in his letters, most notably in his Letter to the Galatians 1:11–24. In many ways, Paul's experience is reminiscent of the calling experiences of some of the prophets, especially Moses (Exod 3:1–12); Isaiah (Isa 6:1–13); Jeremiah (Jer 14–19); and Ezekiel (Ezek 1:1—3:11).

Augustine. *Confessions*. Translated by R. S. Pine-Coffin. Baltimore: Penguin, 1970.

Bainton, Roland H. *Here I Stand: A Life of Martin Luther*. Nashville: Abingdon, 1950.

Muggeridge, Malcolm, ed. *Something Beautiful for God: Mother Teresa's Journey into Compassion*. San Francisco: Harper & Row, 1971.

Outler, Albert C., ed. *John Wesley*, 51–69. New York: Oxford University Press, 1980.

Stendahl, Krister. "Call Rather than Conversion." In *Paul among Jews and Gentiles*, 7–22. Minneapolis: Fortress, 1976.

5

Religion Itself

Progressing in Holiness

Overview and Summary of Content

ALIGNING HIMSELF WITH THE thoughts of Jesus, Methodism's founder John Wesley claimed that true religion is nothing other than loving God and loving the neighbor. More than a simple feeling, loving is an activity. And American Christianity has historically closely followed Wesley by taking the living of religion seriously. In chapter 5, the *Handbook*'s author focuses on Christians' progress in holiness, that is, on Christians' activity of loving, the doing of it. Here is Paul's instruction to the Christians at Corinth: "Love is patient; love is kind; love is not envious or boastful or arrogant or rude. It does not insist on its own way; it is not irritable or resentful; it does not rejoice in wrongdoing but rejoices in the truth. It bears all things, believes all things, hopes all things, endures all things. Love never ends. . . . Pursue love" (1 Cor 13:4–8a; 14:1a).

Christianity's Great Variety

The *Handbook*'s author begins the chapter by reminding us that in some ways, it is easier to speak of Christianities, plural, than Christianity, singular. There is a tremendous variety of views and practices that circulate under the name of the religion. Continuing with a metaphor from earlier chapters, the author discusses Christianity as a large river with various currents. Some Christians and some denominations emphasize certain ones of these currents more than others.

Many Christians emphasize the importance of keeping the ordinances of faith. True Christians, they say, are those who are baptized, who identify themselves as members of a church, who faithfully attend worship services, keep the religious holidays, participate in the Mass or the communion meal, say public prayers, read the Bible, etc. These outward rites serve as visible signs of an inward state of being.

Others place extreme importance on the affirmation of certain core beliefs. True Christians might hold to ancient creedal statements or more recent recitals of tenets considered fundamental to the faith.

Still others have their gaze fixed on heaven. They think of Christians as being aliens in this world, passing through on their way to their true home in heaven.

Some stress the experience of religion, especially the born-again experience. To these, Christianity is all about feeling. The emotion of being assured of salvation and God's love is paramount.

Some Christians emphasize the importance of bringing greater social justice into the world. True Christians are those who are involved perhaps politically to overcome poverty, bring peace, do away with racism, preserve the environment, protect the rights of oppressed groups, etc. Or from the Christian right, true Christians might be those protecting the rights of the unborn or the sanctity of marriage between a man and a woman. These Christians wish to affect the structures of society.

And then, there are other Christians who emphasize doing good deeds but prefer for the influence to be private and individual. Christians are those who feed the hungry, clothe the naked, visit those in prison, or do other acts of charity. Christians are generous, unselfish, good-hearted, compassionate. They tell the truth, are honest, and help others. They don't cheat, lie, drink, or cuss.

Some Emphases for the Twenty-First Century

Christianity, of course, features all six of these characteristics. And it is true, too, that different denominations emphasize some more than others. And to a certain extent, the *Handbook*'s author agrees that all should persist in American Christianity. He mentions keeping the ordinances of the faith, participating in both private aspects of worshiping God such as devoting time each day for prayer, Scripture and religious readings, and meditation, and by becoming members of a community of believers—attending church services, participating in the Lord's Supper, supporting social outreach, etc. He hopes also that twenty-first-century American Protestants continue valuing the traditional creedal statements passed down from the early church. Methodists and American Protestants in general should work at recapturing their roots. They should know shared Christian beliefs. And along with maintaining those links with the beliefs of the past, he urges that some groups of American Protestants need to place more emphasis than currently exists on credentialing aspects of ordination.

Should twenty-first-century Protestants focus on eternity? And should they value a heartwarming experience? Yes, the author answers but hesitantly with the caveat that emotional experiences should not be goals desired in themselves but are valuable when indicating a new state of being.

But what should twenty-first-century Methodists and like-minded Christianity most emphasize? The *Handbook*'s author stresses the importance of a living relationship with Christ. That is, beyond the simple assent to the truth of doctrines, he hopes for greater personal commitment to those essential truths. The focus on eternity, for instance, should not be a turning away from this world but a focusing on the holy that breaks into the world. Christians should be with Christ in the world. And that feeling that accompanies religious experiences should lead to a wholehearted assent to the Lord's demands for how Christians are to live their lives.

Especially important for the author is reaffirming John Wesley's view that believing in Christ means progressing in loving others. Like Paul, Augustine, Martin Luther, and the mainstream of traditional Christianity, Wesley emphasized that believers cannot earn salvation by doing works of charity. God's love is freely given and unmerited. But he also held that whether through political and social involvement to improve the laws and customs of society or through activities wrought by personal holiness, good works follow as night does the day from a relationship with Christ. We love God and love the neighbor because God first loved us. When led by the Spirit, love, joy, peace, patience, kindness, generosity, faithfulness, gentleness, and such would follow.

The Atonement

Why did Jesus have to die? Especially in such a horrible way, crucified like a slave? The *Handbook* points to the traditional answer that through the life and death of Jesus, God reconciled us to himself and all that he had created. Given the human inclination toward evil, we have so alienated ourselves from God, the world, and our own essential selves that if left to our own devices, we would forever remain estranged. God then acted for us.

But couldn't God have brought about a reconciliation without sacrificing his son? After outlining some of the old doctrinal disputes attempting to explain the necessity of God's action, the *Handbook*'s author offers what he thinks essential for twenty-first-century Christians' understanding: The deep point is that the life and death of Christ restores our broken relationship with God, making it possible for us to cooperate with God and prosper in grace. The atonement stresses the great cost to God in overcoming our sinfulness. It shows God's absolute refusal to abandon his creation. Even as mankind has turned ever more inwardly toward the self, God reaches toward us. The ministry of Jesus as well as his death on the cross and his resurrection opened possibilities for a new life in relationship with God.

Atonement Leads to a New Way of Being in the World

The author points out that the atonement further opens the possibility of sanctification or the process of growth that results not solely from Christ but from Christ and humans working together. This was a Wesleyan influence that should continue to mark twenty-first-century American Christianity. A relationship with Christ opens the door to more of God's grace that allows believers to progress in holiness. God's gift of freedom was such that people can backslide into more sin and can even turn their backs completely on God's love. But they can also progress in holiness.

How do we live a holy life that brings true happiness? Methodism started as part of a spiritual revival movement within the Church of England. Under the leadership of Wesley, small groups of Christians would meet regularly, joining in encouragement, prayer, and meditation, seeking together in loving fellowship to lead a more holy life. They adopted rules of attendance and behavior. And the members of the larger Methodist Society and the smaller so-called class meetings would examine, question, advise, and encourage each other first to do no harm, second to do good, and third to attend upon the ordinances of God. Wesley referred to these as fruits that evidenced a desire for salvation.

Where Do We Go from Here?

The *Handbook*'s author ends chapter 5 by focusing on the class meetings of early Methodism. He asks if Christianity can become a philosophy of living and a discipline for us as for those eighteenth-century Methodists. Could it become a task in churches and small discipleship groups to update, contemporize, and bring back into practice the old Methodist General Rules for class and society meetings? He indicates that such a task would call for study of the foundations of our faith and reflection concerning our present state as individuals and a church in light of those foundational events and documents. Moreover, Christian action of doing no harm, doing good, and keeping the ordinances of faith should continually lead back to another round of study, reflection, and new, more faithful activity.

Terms, Dates, Events, and People

Define, identify, or explain each word and phrase as they appear in the *Handbook*'s chapter 5. Ask your instructor or look up words or phrases that remain unclear.

- Christians as aliens in this world
- church trials
- doctrinal standards
- fundamentalism and the Fundamentals of Faith
- God's gift of freedom
- holiness
- infallibility of Scripture
- living relationship with Christ
- ordinances of faith
- orthodoxy
- propitiation
- Revised Common Lectionary
- separatist groups
- Seventh Day Adventists
- *sine qua non* beliefs
- substitutionary atonement
- Unitarian Universalism
- United Societies

Reading Comprehension

Explain these important themes found in chapter 5. Discuss them with course partners. If the *Handbook for the Christian Faith*'s author were in the room with you, what questions would you ask? Can you think of further evidence to buttress the points the author makes?

1. John Wesley claimed that true religion is nothing other than loving God and loving the neighbor. Following this simple insight, Methodists and like-minded Christians take the living of religion seriously. That is, they take the doing of love seriously.

2. Christianity offers various answers to the question of, "What characterizes the true Christian?" The six most common answers recited by the *Handbook*'s author are keeping the ordinances of faith; having right beliefs, or orthodoxy; fixing one's sight on heaven, or otherworldliness; experiencing religion emotionally, especially through the born-again experience; fighting to introduce justice and other Christian values in society, or the social gospel; and living a life commensurate with Christian virtues, or personal holiness. All six ways of being a Christian can be sustained by pointing to Bible passages and the broad river of Christian tradition.

3. Different Christians (and churches) emphasize some of these characteristics more than others. For example, some Christians might place great emphasis on the ordinance of baptism, for example, insisting that the rite is only valid if done in the manner they proscribe, while others accept a variety of baptismal rituals. Or again, some Christians might understand it to be a Christian duty to improve conditions for the poor, perhaps even by campaigning to change laws governing the minimum wage, while others might understand such involvement with secular politics as outside the boundaries of religion.

4. The *Handbook*'s author holds that twenty-first-century American Christians should affirm each of the six characteristics listed but should especially work to recapture the notion of Christianity as a philosophy of living.

5. Beyond a simple assent to the truth of doctrines, Christian living should be characterized by a personal commitment to living those essential truths. That is, generosity, kindness, patience, mercy, justice, and such—in short, the doing of love—should mark Christian living.

6. Good deeds don't bring salvation, but they follow as night does the day from a relationship with Christ. Believing in Christ means progressing in loving others. To be baptized into Christ means to be subsumed into his ways.

7. The atonement holds that the life, death, and resurrection of Christ restored our broken relationship with God, making it possible for us to cooperate with him and prosper in grace. The atonement stresses

the great cost to God in overcoming our sinfulness. It tells us that God refused to abandon us even as we've turned away from him.

8. Christian growth results from joining with Christ to work together. A relationship with Christ opens the door to receiving more of God's grace, a sanctifying grace, that allows believers to progress in holiness.

9. Twenty-first-century Christians should be wary of people who call themselves Christians and yet don't live lives commensurate with Jesus' teachings. Jesus' life, message, and suffering death instruct believers on the path to salvation and wholeness.

10. John Wesley did not intend to start a new church or denomination. Rather, he participated and led a spiritual revival within the Church of England that focused attention on Christian living. The rules governing early Methodist class and society meetings emphasized doing no harm, doing good, and keeping the ordinances of faith. In the eighteenth century, Methodists met regularly in small groups for prayer, exhortation, and to correct and encourage one another in their daily living.

11. The *Handbook*'s author is of the opinion that twenty-first-century Methodists and like-minded Christians have much to gain from rethinking and reestablishing the old Methodist General Rules for class and society meetings. The practice of doing no harm, doing good, and keeping the ordinances of faith, if instituted, would help reconnect American Christianity with that part of itself in danger of being lost, as a philosophy of living for doing love.

Exercises to Enhance Understanding

1. Discuss John Wesley's claim that true religion is nothing other than loving God and loving the neighbor. What does this mean to you? In what ways do you agree or disagree with this perspective? Do you feel that this view of religion is reflected in contemporary Christianity? Why or why not? How and in what ways should Christians strive to be Christ in the world?

2. With other members of your study group, arrange to attend and participate in a worship service at a church or denomination that is different from your own, then spend time reflecting on the experience. What primary differences did you observe in rituals, styles, and the

overall practice of worship? What similarities did you notice? What did you learn?

3. If, as the author suggests, much of American Protestant theology is carried by hymns, is there a dominant theme or pattern you observe in the hymns that are sung and played in your own church? What are some of these hymns? What theological themes or patterns are conveyed in churches that opt for more contemporary or modern music instead of traditional hymns? What are some of the ways music affects our worship experiences?

Suggested Readings

From the Bible: Matthew 5–7; Luke 6:12–49.

Bratcher, Dennis, ed. "The General Rules of the Methodist Class Meetings: The Methodist Church, the Text of 1808 as Amended by Constitutional Actions in 1848 and 1868." *The Voice*, 2018. http://www.crivoice.org/creedclass.html.

Hardt, Philip F. *The Soul of Methodism: The Class Meeting in Early New York City Methodism*. New York: University Press of America, 2000.

Heitzenrater, Richard P. "The Rise of Methodism (1725–39)." In *Wesley and the People Called Methodists*, 37–106. 2nd ed. Nashville: Abingdon, 2013.

Outler, Albert C., ed. *John Wesley*, 119–96. New York: Oxford University Press, 1980.

Williams, Colin W. "The Atonement." In *John Wesley's Theology Today: A Study of the Wesleyan Tradition in the Light of Current Theological Dialogue*, 74–97. Nashville: Abingdon, 1960.

6

Pietism

Overview and Summary of Content

THE FIRST PAGES OF the *Handbook*'s chapter 6 recount the role played by the Moravian Brethren in the development of John Wesley's personal faith. That influence began in the autumn of 1735 when he and his brother Charles were aboard the ship *Simmonds* headed to Georgia and they became friends with Moravian fellow travelers. Spiritual descendants of the martyred Jan Hus, the Moravians had received sanctuary at Herrnhut in today's Germany from the pious Lutheran count Nikolaus Ludwig von Zinzendorf. They gathered in small groups for prayer and Bible reading, put their faith and knowledge of God into practice in daily living, valued the involvement of Christian laypeople in church activities, and expected their pastors to be both well trained and devout. They further emphasized a religion of the heart, the singing of hymns, an ecumenical spirit, the importance of evangelism, and missionary work.

While aboard ship a storm arose, and the Moravians' reaction deeply affected John Wesley. For while Wesley and many of the other passengers were terrified, the Moravians calmly sang hymns, prayed, and showed themselves completely unafraid of death. In his journal, Wesley recounted that he wished for that type of faith and assurance of salvation.

Once in Georgia and then upon Wesley's return to England in 1738, Wesley's friendship with the Moravians grew. And it was through the friendship and influence of a Moravian missionary passing through England on his way to Pennsylvania that Wesley attended the worship at Aldersgate Street Chapel on May 24, 1938, where he felt his heart strangely warmed and saw clearly that he was saved through grace. Wesley continued the association traveling to Herrnhut in August where he experienced the spiritual life of the Moravian congregation and where the joy of religion fully came into his life.

Characteristics of American Religious Piety

Methodists and like-minded evangelicals have always emphasized "doing religion," do no harm, do good, keep the ordinances of faith—but with an essential caveat. The actions must be motivated by love. The Christian seeks a pure heart. Salvation is a state-of-being. And beyond good deeds, that state-of-being includes thoughts, memories, longings, hopes, dispositions. Intentions of the heart walk hand-in-hand with God's grace.

In the class meetings of early Methodism, Wesley and his first followers were striving for no other object than God's love and the desire of pleasing him. And that included living an interior life that showed the fruits of personal salvation. It meant adopting a certain personal lifestyle, governing one's thoughts and plans, seeking every opportunity to do good, undertaking a life of devotion, and living a certain public lifestyle.

Scared into Heaven?

Members of that first group who joined Wesley in society meetings in eighteenth-century England expressed themselves afraid of God's judgment. And most early American Methodists and like-minded Christians too were more interested in being assured of salvation into eternal life than we are. But among Wesley's surviving sermons, only one concerns the terrors of hell, and that one concludes with Wesley thanking God for his mercy that frees us from such merited fate. While Methodism holds to a coming divine judgment, it emphasizes rather the good news of salvation, which isn't received through fear but comes from God's love. And to know God is to respond in love.

Personal Piety in the Public Arena

In those early class meetings, Christians assisted and encouraged one another as each increased in holiness. Participants understood themselves to be cooperating with God's grace, responding to God's love, and entering a relationship with him. Salvation came from God's love, specifically as demonstrated through Christ's atoning death, his life, and teachings; but it was not completely God's choice. Salvation was also an individual choice, an individual response. And salvation required individual responsibility for the life being lived.

Though the early participants envisioned personal piety, their actions naturally overflowed into the public arena. And in truth, the activities of

Christians have never been solely individual and private. Christian responsibility forces certain actions to be no longer private but public. The *Handbook*'s author promises to address social ministry more fully in chapter 14, where he will have more to say also about the separation of church and state. But here, in chapter 6, he points out that a Christian's private and public lives cannot be compartmentalized. Sanctifying grace seeps into the public policy sphere through the lives and activities of believers. Personal decisions with public ramifications are present every day in the typical Christian life.

And some of these private decisions that prove to be not-so-private count among the biggest faith decisions of our lives, and they mark the lives of others, too. There is no hiding from the problems that ensue. The author provides examples, retelling the story of a few White ministers who in 1963 took a public stand against racism in segregated Mississippi, of the cost of a German Lutheran's discipleship to Christ in Nazi Germany in 1945, and of the witness of a Presbyterian liberation theologian against the murder of priests teaching Central American *campesinos* what was in the Bible in the 1980s. The author asks, what issues do we support politically? How do we react to abuse and violence? Which causes do we help mobilize? What charities do we help fund? Where and how do we spend our money? What jobs do we hold? How do we interact with others and God's creation? For Christ himself forces his followers off the sidelines into the ballgame.

Christian Perfection

The author ends the chapter with a discussion of Wesley's view that Christians should be progressing toward perfection. In keeping with the Greek of the New Testament, Wesley understood Christian perfection somewhat differently than do many Americans. To him, perfection didn't mean "without blemish," "without fault," "infallible," but rather "being complete," "reaching a designated purpose," "being whole," "mature," "full-grown." Wesley's idea was that Christians could and should progress in love to that level of holiness or sanctity intended by God for humans from creation. This differed from Roman Catholicism of his day where Christian holiness had become stylized into vows of obedience, poverty, and chastity and works of supererogation. And it also differed from the Calvinists and Anglicans of that time who thought that perfection was only possible to the elect after death, in heaven once the body was glorified. His view recaptured that of some of the church fathers, however, who thought of the Christian life as a journey on the way to holiness.

For Wesley, Christian perfection meant being freed of self-will, wishing only the holy will of God. Ideally, the Christian would advance in sanctity to the point where sin as a willful act ceased. And for him, in fact, it was in order to call Christians to the possibility of full sanctification that God allowed for the formation of the people called Methodists. It was in placing aside this particular early church doctrine that the Reformation had fallen short, he thought. And following Wesley and those first Methodists, the *Handbook*'s author urges twenty-first-century Americans to revitalize this aspect of Christianity and to more closely follow early Christianity and the teachings of Jesus in the Sermon on the Mount, for instance, in holding that believers can progress in holiness.

But there are dangers that accompany the whole Christian perfection movement. The author reminds Christians that they would do well to avoid the trap of confusing God's blessings of health, wealth, recognition, power, accomplishments, etc., with holiness. There is the potential of emphasizing individual religion to the exclusion of the community. And obviously Christians would be wrong to confuse true holiness with a *feeling* of being holy.

Moreover, for some the emotional outbursts that at times accompanied Christian perfection became the hallmark of their religion. Emotional manifestations accompanied the power that arrived with the Holy Spirit and freedom from sin. But orderliness in worship and a rational theology were in the eighteenth century and continue today to be truer characteristics of American Methodism and established Protestantism.

Where Do We Go from Here?

The *Handbook*'s author ends chapter 6 by reaffirming that Wesley was right when he exhorted Christians to emphasize holiness. The realization that we are all sinners and fall short of the glory of God (Rom 3:23) can become an excuse (for us and our church) for living separate from God. Sanctification is nothing more than putting God and the other first and putting ourselves, our desires, our accomplishments, last. Loving God manifests itself in loving the neighbor.

Terms, Dates, Events, and People

Define, identify, or explain each word and phrase as they appear in the *Handbook*'s chapter 6. Ask your instructor or look up words or phrases that remain unclear.

- Charles Wesley
- class meetings and band meetings
- Dietrich Bonhoeffer and *The Cost of Discipleship*
- divine judgment
- ecumenical spirit
- Establishment Clause of the First Amendment
- holiness movement
- Jonathan Edwards
- liberation theology
- meaning of Christian perfection
- Moravian Brethren
- personal holiness
- rational theology
- religious piety
- sanctification
- sanctuary movement
- *United Methodist Book of Discipline*

Reading Comprehension

Explain these important themes found in chapter 6. Discuss them with course partners. If the *Handbook for the Christian Faith*'s author were in the room with you, what questions would you ask? Can you think of further evidence to buttress the points the author makes?

1. John Wesley, Methodism, and American Protestantism in general were deeply influenced by the Moravian Brethren.

2. Historically, pietism stressed having Christian laypersons read and study the Bible, involve themselves in all church activities, practice their faith in daily living, and approach religious controversies and discussion with humility and love. Pastors were to be well-trained and devout, and they were expected to orient their sermons toward developing the faith of believers. Pietism emphasized a religion of the

heart, singing hymns, holding an ecumenical spirit, evangelism, and missionary work.

3. Methodists and like-minded Christians have emphasized personal holiness and doing religion. Christians seek a pure heart. Actions of charity are to be motivated by love.

4. The *Handbook*'s author claims that salvation is a state of being. Beyond deeds, the state of being includes thoughts, memories, longings, hopes, and dispositions.

5. Methodists and like-minded Protestants hold that no act of kindness, no demonstration of holiness, and no religious activity are sufficient to merit God's grace.

6. Good deeds should be motivated by the pure act of loving God, the neighbor, and God's creation. Intentions of the heart walk hand-in-hand with God's grace. We are able to love because God first loved us. God's love leads us to want to do good and live a life pleasing to him.

7. Eighteenth- and nineteenth-century European-Americans generally exhibited more urgency than modern Christians to flee the righteous anger deserved on God's accounting day. While continuing to affirm a coming judgment day, present-day Methodists and like-minded Christians follow Wesley in emphasizing God's love and saving grace. Wellness does not come through fear. God is love. To know God is to respond in love.

8. In early Methodist society and class meetings, Christians assisted and encouraged one another as they increased in holiness. They understood themselves to be cooperating with God's sanctifying grace, responding to his love, and entering a relationship with him.

9. Even when so intended, the activities of Christians are not solely individual and private. Loving actions have social ramifications. Christian actions naturally overflow into the public arena.

10. Personal decisions which carry public implications are present every day in the typical Christian life. Religious views do not only bleed into public life; they force Christians inexorably to make certain public decisions.

11. John Wesley recaptured the thought of many early church fathers who considered the Christian life to be a journey on the way to holiness. Wesley understood Jesus to have instructed his followers to reach the sanctity intended by God for humans from creation. For Wesley, Christian perfection meant being freed from self-will and wishing

only to be guided by the holy will of God. He thought that Christians could reach that type of perfection while alive.

12. For some followers of Wesley, Christian perfection became the hallmark of their religion. There were times and places where the holiness movement morphed into an extreme emotionalism with which Wesley and most Methodists and like-minded Christians feel uncomfortable. Wesley and most of his followers have emphasized rationality and orderly worship.

Exercises to Enhance Understanding

1. Philipp Jakob Spener's *Pia Desideria* was influential in the formation of the movement known as pietism. In pairs or in small groups, discuss your thoughts on Spener's six strategies for reform that emphasized prayer and Bible reading over dogma. These strategies are listed on pages 114–15 of the text. In what ways do you find these strategies helpful? In what ways do you see or not see these strategies reflected in the modern church? How might they be helpful for the challenges faced by the contemporary church? What strategies would you add to this list?

2. The class meetings and band meetings of early Methodism provided a form of accountability for Christians who were striving to live a life that was pleasing to God and that was reflective of God's love. What groups or communities are you a part of that offer such means of accountability for your own Christian life? In what ways does your participation in these groups hold you accountable to doing good and to keeping the ordinances of God? Are such groups necessary for the development of piety or religious faith? Are there any ways the contemporary church might be impacted by the utilization of small groups similar to the early Methodist classes and bands?

3. The author states that the activities of Christians have never been solely individual or private and points out that John Wesley instructed Christians to vote and to respect and speak no ill of those they vote against or of those on the opposing side. In what ways do Christians follow or ignore these instructions in contemporary American politics? Do you think Christians continue to have a responsibility to vote and to be respectful of those with whom they disagree? Why or why

not? Why do you think political discourse in America today does not seem to reflect Wesley's instructions?

Suggested Readings

Carter, Henry. "Along the Road that Brought Them to the Inheritance." In *The Methodist Heritage*, 34–58. Nashville: Abingdon-Cokesbury, 1951.

———. "They Explore the Inheritance in Controversies and Discussions." In *The Methodist Heritage*, 59–90. Nashville: Abingdon-Cokesbury, 1951.

Ferré. Nels F. S. "God Can Be Experienced." In *Methodism: A Summary of Basic Information Concerning the Methodist Church*, edited William K. Anderson, 116–27. Nashville: Methodist, 1947.

Harris, Franklin Rall. "The Search for Perfection." In *Methodism: A Summary of Basic Information Concerning the Methodist Church*, edited William K. Anderson, 139–48. Nashville: Methodist, 1947.

Heitzenrater, Richard P. "Methodism and the Christian Heritage in England." In *Wesley and the People Called Methodists*, 18–36. 2nd ed. Nashville: Abingdon, 2013.

Hutton, James E. *A History of the Moravian Church*. 1895. Reprint, Columbia, SC: Pantianos Classics, 2016.

Thomas à Kempis. *The Imitation of Christ Selections*. Translated by Aloysius Croft and Harold Bolton. Milwaukee: Bruce, 1940. Originally published ca. 1400. Christian Classics Ethereal Library. http://www.ccel.org/ccel/kempis/imitation.html.

Wesley, John. *A Plain Account of Christian Perfection*. London: Epworth, 1952.

Williams, Colin W. "The Order of Salvation: Christian Perfection." In *John Wesley's Theology Today: A Study of the Wesleyan Tradition in the Light of Current Theological Dialogue*, 167–90. Nashville: Abingdon, 1960.

7

The Scriptures

Overview and Summary of Content

IN PART III OF the *Handbook for the Christian Faith* the author tackles the question of how people come to know the truth about God, themselves, and their intended relationship with the world. He suggests that there are several roads to reaching ultimate truth. However, all of Christianity agrees that clearest insight into the nature of God comes through the life, teachings, ministry, suffering-death, and resurrection of Jesus Christ. But few lived in first-century Galilee during the days of Jesus. So, how does God reveal his nature and the nature of creation to all people even when they perhaps have never heard of Christ? In the first chapter of Part III, chapter 7, the author focuses on the Scriptures.

The Bible Leads Us to Truth

Though an avid reader of many books, John Wesley placed special value on the Bible and even referred to himself as a person of only one book. He considered the Scriptures inspired by God and to be followed in all matters of religion and morality, if clearly enjoined or forbidden. All things necessary for salvation were contained in Scripture. And Methodists and like-minded Protestants have followed Wesley in affirming that hearing the word of God is enough to bring a person to an understanding of the human situation and God's grace. Through the stories and teachings in the Bible, God can lead us to see both who we currently are and who God wishes us to be. Hearing the Word of God opens the possibility for new life.

The Bible as a Place Christians Live

The *Handbook*'s author recounts a wonderful parable from the Bible scholar Carlos Mesters describing how the antiquity of the Bible joined with the work of scholars and the reverence given to the writings to distance Scripture from the everyday life of believers. In the parable, Mesters compared the Bible with a house that became over time something like a museum. But unexpectedly, poor people rediscovered the Bible as a place that brought protection from the cold and where they could sing and dance. Powerfully, the parable distinguished the word of God as "a place where people live" from the word of God as "a place (or object) that scholars study."

The author's point in retelling Mesters's parable is that it recaptures much of early Christianity's view and Wesley's view that Scripture is not a dead word but a living word. Moreover, Scripture has life and gives life only so long as it is a lived reality.

The Reformation's Approach to Scripture

Wesley's approach to the Bible grew out of the Reformation where Martin Luther and others lessened the authority of church tradition and heightened the authority of the Scriptures and clear reason. When turning to Scripture, Luther assumed certain things about it. He assumed that Scripture itself was the best interpreter of Scripture, meaning that the best way to understand a confusing passage in the Bible was by turning to another passage where the meaning was clear. He assumed that Scripture spoke with one voice and that its meaning must be plain and clear.

But the problem, of course, was that the Bible itself could not support the weight of these expectations. Thus, Luther and the earliest Reformers added the proclamation of Christ as a hermeneutic principle. Christ, his life, teachings, passion, and resurrection, became the key to unlocking the meaning of the Scriptures. The Old Testament or covenant was to be rightly understood through the hearing aid of the New Testament. The Reformers used typology. All of history pointed forward and backward to Christ. Further, Luther and his fellow Reformers adopted the notion that the word of God and the Bible were distinct. The word of God occurred in the hearing of Scripture. Moreover, they thought of the Holy Spirit leading the hearing of individual readers, inspiring them. It was less active in the corrupt councils of the Roman church. The work of the Holy Spirit affected not only the interpretation of passages but the selection of books to be included in the Christian canon. Luther himself separated the apocryphal (or deuterocanonical) books into the middle section of his German language Bible. And Article V of Wesley's Twenty-five Articles of Religion, following closely to Article VI of the Church of England's Thirty-nine Articles, does not include the apocryphal books among the books of the Bible. Luther and the early Reformers accepted the church's long emphasis on scholarship, studied Greek and Hebrew, and soon moved Bible reading away from the Latin into the vernacular.

Wesley and the Word of God

Like the Protestant Reformers of the sixteenth century, Wesley distinguished the word of God from the Bible. Christ was the word of God. The gospel was the word of God. Whatever proclaims Christ is the word of God.

Although contours remained similar, by Wesley's day the Enlightenment and world travel had led Protestant exegetes to become both more and less sophisticated about hermeneutics than in the earliest heady days of the Reformation. One sees the question of genre in Wesley's comments. Wesley and his Anglican colleagues did not read the Bible searching for answers to scientific problems or right government. But also, with Anglican evangelicalism in the eighteenth century, Bible reading had become more private, more individual, less community oriented. For Wesley, the Bible was a religious book that told how to find the way to heaven. It illuminated the love of God and offered a guide for the Christian's journey toward greater holiness. Also with Wesley, we don't see the defensiveness that marked early reactions to the Enlightenment's attack on the supernatural. And Wesley also helped with the irreconcilable differences in Scripture that so puzzled Deists and Enlightenment figures like John Toland and Hermann Samuel Reimarus and continue to be the bane of literalism today. Twenty-first-century American Christians should follow Wesley's lead in holding that it is quite okay to ask Scripture hard questions.

Wesley had the habit of constantly reading the Bible, both in serious study and in meditation. Akin to Mesters's parable, he thought in terms of living with the Bible, reading it constantly in study and meditation. He was convinced that when doing so, those matters that are essential would come to the fore. Matters that are nonessential would fade to background. Once developing the practice of reading the Bible constantly and reading the Old Testament through the lens of the gospel, there was little chance of being confused about the message of God's love and his expectations and hope for our love.

Using the Tools of Scholarship

Like Luther and many of the Reformers, Wesley was a strong scholar. But the *Handbook*'s author asks us to recognize that the tools and science of exegesis have progressed since Wesley's day, offering twenty-first-century ministers many advantages unforeseen in former times. We have a much better grasp of the history and culture of the first century, of its social world, language, and customs and are more keenly aware of how different our worldview is from theirs of the first century. Also, ministers today are trained in accredited seminaries not to assume that a naïvely literal understanding of the text recaptures what the original hearers heard. When Wesley approached the Bible, as an exegete his focus was narrow. He read in large measure to uncover what the Scriptures said concerning the way to heaven. In many ways, his was a private reading. The Bible was a guide to the individual's pilgrimage to a more holy relationship with God. This is quite different than the approach of the twenty-first-century exegete whose goal is to locate the intended meaning of the text. Using form, redaction, audience, and literary criticisms; source and synoptic theories; and all historical-critical tools, the minister seeks to locate the meaning true to the writing's time and place, and then allow that meaning to be proclaimed in today's world.

Where Do We Go from Here?

The author concludes chapter 7 by urging Christians to form the habit of reading the Bible. That they should read it from beginning to end, read it constantly, and trust that those things that are essential for faith will come through. The author also urges scholarly study. Deep knowledge of the biblical writings' social and historical contexts can add much to our understanding. And he is of the opinion that clergy and others with special training have a special responsibility to help laypersons with such studies.

Terms, Dates, Events, and People

Define, identify, or explain each word and phrase as they appear in the *Handbook*'s chapter 7. Ask your instructor or look up words or phrases that remain unclear.

- Christ as best insight into the nature of God
- apocryphal books of the Bible
- centrality of Scripture

- concept of inerrancy
- Diet of Worms
- doctrine of purgatory
- eschatology
- form criticism and redaction criticism
- hermeneutics and exegesis
- the incarnation
- knowability of God
- literalist understanding of the Bible
- miracle and mystery of the resurrection
- natural theology
- Paulo Freire and *Pedagogy of the Oppressed*
- Scripture as life-giving and lived reality
- social reversal
- source theory
- textual criticism
- the word of God

Reading Comprehension

Explain these important themes found in chapter 7. Discuss them with course partners. If the *Handbook for the Christian Faith*'s author were in the room with you, what questions would you ask? Can you think of further evidence to buttress the points the author makes?

1. The *Handbook*'s author suggests that while there are alternate approaches to knowing truth, some paths to perceiving God and our intended relation with him and creation are better than others. All of Christianity agrees that our clearest insight into the nature of God comes through Jesus Christ, his life, teachings, ministry, suffering-death, and resurrection.

2. Christians hold that the coming of Christ established the possibility again of having a deep relationship between creator and creature that sin had taken away.

3. Martin Luther and other sixteenth-century Reformers moved away from church tradition and the authority of church councils. Seeking to return to the greater purity of early Christianity, they turned to Scripture and clear reason.

4. Martin Luther in the sixteenth century and Wesley in the eighteenth century distinguished the word of God from the Bible. Christ was the word of God. The gospel was the word of God. Whatever proclaims Christ is the word of God.

5. Hearing the word of God in the Bible uncovers both what a person has become and what God wishes that person to be. Hearing the word of God opens the possibility for new life.

6. As recounted in the *Handbook*, Carlos Mesters's Parable of the House distinguished the word of God as a place where people live from the word of God as an object that scholars study. Scripture has life and gives life only so long as it is a lived reality.

7. Reading and discussing the exodus story in the Old Testament and Jesus' proclamation of social reversal in Luke 6 can prove liberating to oppressed people. But also, it can present a dangerous threat to powerful people who benefit from systems of oppression.

8. Like Martin Luther, John Wesley thought that the word of God spoke clearly and with one voice. But that did not mean he thought the Bible writings were inerrant in scientific matters, for instance, or economic matters, or political matters—or even that they agreed in detail. From earliest times, careful readers of the Bible have been aware of great differences, even contradictions, in the biblical accounts. There are four gospels in the canon, not just one, because they are different, not because they say the same thing.

9. John Wesley held that the Scriptures were inspired by God. In matters of religion the Scriptures were to be followed. Matters of morality, if clearly enjoined, were to be followed. All things necessary for salvation were contained in Scripture. For Wesley the Bible was a religious book that told how to find the way to heaven. It illuminated the love of God and offered a guide for the Christian's journey toward greater holiness.

10. For twenty-first-century Christians, the author advocates the practice of reading the Bible constantly in study and meditation. When doing so, those matters that are essential will come to the fore. Matters that are nonessential will fade into the background.

11. Study and deep knowledge of the biblical writings' social and historical contexts can help us see how early Christians understood the texts. The tools of modern biblical scholarship locate the text's meaning in the time and place of original composition. From the pulpit, the minister translates and proclaims that message for today's world.

Exercises to Enhance Understanding

1. Read 2 Timothy 3:16–17. This is a well-known and oft-quoted passage about the importance of Scripture.[1] Given what you have read and learned in chapter 7, do these verses mean something new or different to you now? What does it mean for Scripture to be inspired by God? How does this understanding shape your own theological perspective? In your own congregation, how is Scripture understood to be inspired by God?

2. What are your earliest memories about how the Bible was viewed in your church and your family? Did Scripture and learning stories from the Bible play a significant role? How has your view of the importance of Scripture—both as it is used in corporate worship and in your own devotional life—evolved or changed over time?

3. The author points to the multiple Easter stories in the Bible to illustrate differences in Scripture that defy a literalist interpretation. In pairs or in small groups, discuss other examples of differences seen in multiple versions of stories from the Bible, such as in the creation accounts in Genesis or in the death of Goliath. What are the implications for your own faith and understanding of Scripture given that the Bible offers us multiple versions of stories? What challenging or difficult questions does this raise for you? In what ways does it enhance the meanings or understandings we draw from Scripture?

---

1. The 2 Tim 3:16–17 passage holds two translation difficulties: 1) The Greek may be translated "*all Scripture is inspired* by God and is profitable"; or, it may be translated "*all Scripture that is inspired* is profitable" [italics added]. Both readings are grammatically correct. And 2) the letter to Timothy was written before the establishment of a New Testament canon. Does, then, the Scripture mentioned refer to the Hebrew Bible only? Or did the writer also have in mind some New Testament writings? And if so, which?

Suggested Readings

Bruce, Frederick F. *The New Testament Documents: Are They Reliable?* Grand Rapids: Eerdmans, 1943, paperback, 2003.

Burtner, Robert W., and Robert Chiles, eds. "Religious Knowledge and Authority." In *A Compend of Wesley's Theology*, 15–22. Nashville: Abingdon, 1954.

Dawsey, James M. "The Lost Front Door into Scripture: The Church Fathers and Latin American Biblical Interpretation." *The Anglican Theological Review* 72.3 (1990) 292–305.

Greenslade, Stanley L., ed. *The West from the Reformation to the Present Day*. The Cambridge History of the Bible 3. Cambridge: Cambridge University Press, 1963.

Kümmel, Werner Georg. *The New Testament: The History of the Investigation of Its Problems*. Translated by S. McLean Gilmour and Howard C. Kee. Nashville: Abingdon, 1972.

Origen. *On First Principles*. Translated by G. W. Butterworth. New York: Harper & Row, 1966.

Outler, Albert C., ed. "Doctrinal Summaries." In *John Wesley*, 171–82. New York: Oxford University Press, 1980.

8

Church History, Reason, and Christian Experience

Natural Theology

Overview and Summary of Content

CHAPTER 8 OF THE *Handbook for the Christian Faith* focuses on how God's truth is available to every person—not just to those who happened to be present when Jesus walked the earth in Galilee and Judea, and not just to those exposed to God's word through the Scriptures. Methodists and like-minded Christians affirm that his truth is available through reason and other natural means, through secular history, also through the activity of the church universal, and through the lives of everyday, but sometimes exceptional human beings.

Secular History?

One way to read the Bible is as the memory of God's mighty acts. The biblical story is not told as might a journalist, trying to record the who, why, where, when of events. And its focus is not on military, economic, or political events. The telling is not scientific. Rather the Bible's story is told through the eyes of faith. It starts with pre-history, telling of God's ordering of chaos into our universe and how he created humans in his own image and likeness and was greatly concerned for their wellbeing. It tells of people's disobedience and, shifting from pre-history to history more properly, recounts the consequences that followed. And it tells of God's relationship with our ancestors and his utter refusal to abandon his creation. It tells of his love for us.

Events were selected, interpreted, and related by a community of faith. And for those within that community. The story gives deep insight into the nature of God and his creation.

Twenty-first-century American Protestants and Secular History

Christians affirm that the coming of Christ marked a turning point in history, not its end, and that God continues active in the events of secular history. And Methodists and like-minded Christians believe that God's Holy Spirit remains active in events of today. The basic pattern of Sunday worship typically begins with an invocation recognizing God's continuing presence and activity. And all but a few American Christian churches celebrate not just religious holy days, like Easter and Christmas, but national holidays. God is active in American history. The church rituals celebrate God's saving activity in our history. God is invoked as a protector of the nation and of humanity. God is present, blesses, and brings correction, justice, and mercy to the contemporary world.

The *Handbook*'s author points out that while certain Christian values have become part of the ethos of our nation, Article 1 of the United States Bill of Rights declares that Congress "will make no law regarding the establishment of religion or prohibiting the free exercise thereof." Methodists and like-minded American Christians affirm that the state should protect individual conscience; that religion lies between the person and her or his god. All religions that are not dangerous to individuals or the nation should be tolerated. And the self-examination of one's own faith that follows toleration strengthens true religion.

The History of the Church Universal

God reveals himself and his truth beyond secular history through the history of the church universal as led by the Holy Spirit. The Reformation, the 1563 Convocation of the Church of England by Elizabeth I, the Barmen Declaration, Vatican II, and the Papal encyclical *Laudato si* are examples of God's activities in the world through the church. God is active also in the founding of church-related colleges and universities; the building and staffing of hospitals, orphanages, and care facilities; through home and foreign missions; through relief organizations; and through countless other institutions and agencies. And sometimes, God uses the church to stand against governments that are leading society in ways contrary to his desires.

Wesley's and his eighteenth-century Church of England evangelical contemporaries' use of British law to abolish slavery is an example.

Individual History

And finally, as regards history, God's truth can be perceived by observing his actions in the history of individuals. These might be famous religious figures like Mother Teresa of Calcutta, Saint Damien of Molokai, or John Wesley himself. But most often, they are people who we see every day—family, friends, fellow Christian churchmen and women. And the author urges that we never underestimate our own witness as Christian models.

Reason

The mainstream of Christianity has always held that the human mind can lead us to truth. The Gospel of John begins not with a birth narrative but with a hymn connecting the coming of Jesus to the word of creation. And the *Handbook*'s author explains that *Logos* or word also denoted rational thought in antiquity. *Logos* was the common Greek word for reason, motive, and plan. There was a rational force at work in creation. Physical and biological laws govern the universe and our world. God's organizing of chaos at creation was a rational undertaking. And since humans were created in the image of God, that is, imbued with reason, we were created with the ability to understand creation and much about God. Humans were created such that we can observe events, discern cause and effect, analyze problems, draw conclusions, perform physical and mind experiments, discover solutions, and record our discoveries. In teams, we can build on the discoveries that preceded us and pass our own contributions forward to the next generations. If we are thinking correctly, our thinking parallels God's. We can grasp truth with our minds.

While some few groups of Christians have shunned education, thinking that schooling and any reading beyond the Bible to be a corrupting influence that destroys childhood innocence and places the human soul in danger, Methodists and like-minded Protestants think differently. Ignorance, rather, leads to prejudice and human arrogance. It results from laziness. It belittles God's gift to us of a mind. It interferes with our ability to help others. It deprecates God's commands that we look after his creation and love our neighbor.

Christian Experience, Feelings, Emotions

For Methodists and the like-minded, reason and emotion work in tandem in Christian experience. Christian feeling energizes the believer to love, to speak, to do the truth. As there is no love outside the act of love, there is no truth separate from the doing of it. A good sermon moves both the mind and the heart toward a closer relationship with the Lord.

The author asks us also to consider the role that singing plays in worship, for hymns move mind and heart. For John Wesley, hymn singing filled an emotional need of the heart to praise God and be close to Christ. He loved singing and held definite views about hymns and their function in the church. He emphasized congregational participation. He expected the congregation to sing as if one, in a united voice, no person louder or distinct from another, for the congregation was to be one in Christ. He also placed importance on the words of the hymns. The hymns, for Wesley, carried the theology of the church.

Emotionalism

Toward the end of the chapter, the *Handbook*'s author inserts a caution, urging American Protestants to be careful with unrestrained enthusiasm. He points out that in Wesley's *Journal*, Wesley showed ambivalence toward spiritual manifestations and that in general, his descriptions are nonjudgmental. But whenever the manifestations became the focal point of worship, Wesley moved his congregations away from them. The author then described a series of events where emotional intensity reached such height that it dominated meetings, caused division among the worshipers, and gave license for some to feel superior to others. For Wesley, feeling for its own sake, emotionalism, was a tune without words. The heart strangely warmed should energize us to live the truth, he thought—to love God, love our neighbor, and care for all things entrusted to us. As the melody in hymns accompanies a text, emotion should accompany reason. Emotions in worship, as in life, should always attend to the message of God's word.

Where Do We Go from Here?

The author concludes chapter 8 by challenging churches to do more than instruct congregations about the Bible. The Christian heritage includes also theology, church history, ethics, and other matters. He suggests that local churches dedicate time on their calendars to offering classes, workshops,

CHURCH HISTORY, REASON, AND CHRISTIAN EXPERIENCE 67

training, and lectures in these areas also. Christians should take seriously Jesus' instruction that his followers love God also with their minds. And he promises that bringing a better understanding of the Christian heritage to parishioners will benefit parishioners and local congregations in many ways. Better training in the essentials of the faith will help believers prioritize their lives within the tradition of faith.

Terms, Dates, Events, and People

Define, identify, or explain each word and phrase as they appear in the *Handbook*'s chapter 8. Ask your instructor or look up words or phrases that remain unclear.

- church as prophetic voice
- council of bishops
- dialectic
- emotionalism
- faith as an individualized endeavor
- Isaac Watts
- Jesus as representative of Adam, Moses, Joshua, David, and others
- John Winthrop's image of a "city upon a hill"
- *logos*
- manifestations of the Spirit
- messiah and understanding of kingship
- Methodist Episcopal Church, South
- nonconformists
- Plato
- preaching as both a rational and emotive exercise
- reason as a gift from God
- religious history
- Social Principles of the United Methodist Church
- United Methodist Committee on Relief
- Yahweh

Reading Comprehension

Explain these important themes found in chapter 8. Discuss them with course partners. If the *Handbook for the Christian Faith*'s author were in the room with you, what questions would you ask? Can you think of further evidence to buttress the points the author makes?

1. Most Christians hold that God's truth is evident through natural means available to every human being. Besides through the life, teachings, death, and resurrection of Jesus Christ and through the Scriptures, God reveals himself through creation, history, reason, and experience.

2. One way to read the Bible is as the memory of God's mighty acts. The biblical story is not scientific and is not written as history found in academic books of history. Rather, events were selected, interpreted, and told by a community of faith.

3. Christians affirm that the coming of Christ marked a turning point in history, not its end. God continues to be active in secular history. And his Holy Spirit is active in the church today.

4. Christians also can perceive truth by observing God's actions in the lives and history of individuals. These might be famous religious figures. But common are Christians we see every day. You and I should never underestimate our own witness as Christian models.

5. Article 1 of the Bill of Rights declares that the United States "will make no law regarding the establishment of religion or prohibiting the free exercise thereof." Following John Locke, Methodists and like-minded Protestants affirm that the state should protect individual conscience; that religion lies between the person and his or her god. All religions that are not dangerous to individuals or the nation should be tolerated. And the self-examination of one's own faith that follows toleration strengthens true religion.

6. Following Jesus and the Apostle Paul, the mainstream of Christianity has always held that the human mind can lead to truth. Since humans were created in the image and likeness of God, our minds allow us (if we are thinking correctly) to understand God's creation and purposes.

7. Jesus asked that we love God with our minds. Such entails the obligations both to develop the gifts of reason, critical thinking, study, knowledge, etc., and to apply the understanding that follows to further God's purposes.

8. Methodists and like-minded Christians recognize science as a legitimate interpretation of God's natural world and affirm the validity of the claims of science in describing the natural world. But at the same time, theological understandings of human experience are crucial to a full understanding of the place of humanity in the universe. Science and theology are complementary rather than mutually incompatible.

9. Reason and emotion work in tandem in Christian experience. Christian feelings energize believing, loving, speaking, and doing the truth. As there is no love outside the act of love, there is no truth separate from the doing of it.

10. For Wesley, hymn singing filled an emotional need of the heart to praise God and be close to Christ. Wesley emphasized congregational hymn singing as it enhanced worship as a communal activity. He also gave great importance to the words of the hymns as they carried the theology of the church. Emotions cooperated with reason to bring individual singers and the congregation closer to Christ.

11. Wesley and early Methodism were ambivalent about manifestations of the spirit. But whenever these manifestations became the focal point of worship, Wesley moved the Methodist societies away from them. Overt emotionalism, he thought, disrupted the orderliness and common sense that should mark society meetings. It led to irrationality. Emotion in worship, as in life, should attend to the message of God's word.

Exercises to Enhance Understanding

1. In this chapter, the author discusses the events of creation as a story told by a community of faith. The biblical story is not intended to be a scientific or historical story. In pairs or in groups, discuss the ways our understanding of the scientific world and our understanding of Scripture inform one another. What are examples from your daily life that illustrate the way these two perspectives coexist together? In what ways does religious faith impact our scientific understanding of the world? In what ways does our scientific understanding of the world impact our religious faith? Are the two compatible or mutually exclusive?

2. In your own congregation and church, what do you see as examples of the way patriotism and religious faith are entwined? What role should patriotism play in our worship, if any? The United Methodist Hymnal contains songs such as "America" and "America the Beautiful."

American flags are present in most sanctuaries. Memorials to church members who lost their lives in wars and through military service can be found in many churches. What are ways you have witnessed patriotism displayed or discussed in a worship setting that seem appropriate and done with integrity?

3. The singing of hymns played a significant role in the theology and worship practices of John and Charles Wesley. See if you can find John Wesley's "Directions for Singing" in *The United Methodist Hymnal*. Have you ever noticed these instructions before? [The author also lists the directions on pages 171 and 172 of the text.] In pairs or in a group, discuss your understanding of the directive from Wesley to "Above all sing spiritually. . . ." What does this mean to you?

Suggested Readings

Burtner, Robert W., and Robert Chiles, eds. "Religious Knowledge and Authority." In *A Compend of Wesley's Theology*, 23–40. Nashville: Abingdon, 1954.

Clarke, Martin V. "John Wesley's 'Directions for Singing': Methodist Hymnody as an Expression of Methodist Beliefs in Thought and Practice." *Methodist History* 47.4 (July 2009) 196–209.

Hume, David. *David Hume: Dialogues Concerning Natural Religion and the Posthumous Essays*. Edited by Richard H. Popkin. Cambridge: Hackett, 1980.

Lewis, Clive S. *Mere Christianity*. New York: Harper Collins, 1952.

Locke, John. "A Letter Concerning Toleration." The Federalist Papers Project, edited by Steve Straub, June 2, 2011. https://thefederalistpapers.org/wp-content/uploads/2012/12/John-Locke-A-Letter-Concerning-Toleration.pdf.

Outler, Albert C. "The Wesleyan Quadrilateral in Wesley." *Wesleyan Theological Journal* 20.1 (Spring 1985) 7–18.

Williams, Colin W. "Authority and Experience." In *John Wesley's Theology Today: A Study of the Wesleyan Tradition in the Light of Current Theological Dialogue*, 23–38. Nashville: Abingdon, 1960.

9

The History of Methodist Women

Overview and Summary of Content

PART IV OF THE *Handbook for the Christian Faith* concerns Methodism's mixed record satisfying Christianity's ideal of brotherhood and sisterhood. The author introduces the section by reminding us that all people are descended from Adam and Eve and considered daughters and sons of God. Christianity treasures the thought of an extensive family of God. And yet, this is an area where the religion has fallen short of what it professes and at times has practiced an ugly exclusion. And unfortunately, Methodists and like-minded Christians count among those who have too often betrayed their own affirmations. Chapter 9 is about Christians' historical battle for the inclusion of women.

American Religion and the Women's Movement

The author admits without defensiveness that the movement for sexual and gender equality in our nation has been disappointingly slow. Mentioning Anne Hutchinson and Mary Dyer as early battlers for the spiritual equality of women in America, he turns to the key role played by Quaker women during the fight for social justice including ultimately the right to vote that marked the first wave of the women's movement. Courage and belief in spiritual equality have been telltale marks of Quakers. And several Quakers were active in organizing the 1848 Seneca Falls Convention, founding the National Women's Suffrage Association, launching women's rights publications, and leading the final push for suffrage.

But as the author points out, Christians from many different denominations participated in the nineteenth- and early twentieth-century push for women's rights—and there were also participants and leaders who were not Christians. While many activists of that first wave were motivated by sentiments intertwined with their Christian faith, the women's movement did not spring from Christianity. Some of the strongest opposition to women's rights was mounted by Christian churches. And this fact is even more pronounced with the so-called second wave feminism of the 1960s and '70s and successive waves that have had at most tangential ties to the Christian community. In fact, the second wave with its emphases on expanding sexual and reproductive rights and women's work outside the home received strong pushback from conservative Christians, including Christian women arguing that men were intended by God to be the spiritual leaders, protectors, breadwinners, decision makers, and heads of the family.

Class Meetings in Early Methodism

The author turns attention to the original Methodist societies and discovers something interesting. Women played an important role in the development of early Methodism. Women outnumbered men by near two-to-one ratio in membership records. The women, who came from diverse social strata—in America, both White and Black—joined the societies between the ages of sixteen and twenty-four. Furthermore, the Methodist women played a strong leadership role in early Methodism.

It was in class meeting leadership where women most shone. The classes were groups of friends and family, young, old, women, men, poor, and well-to-do that would meet for Christian fellowship in homes, or once built, Methodist chapels. Sometimes in those early days, the group would be gender specific, only women or only men; sometimes not. The congregants would pray, sing hymns, testify to God's work in their lives, share their hopes and doubts, and assist one another. Participants were encouraged to speak openly about their spiritual journey. The classes would also raise money to build chapels, help the poor, and support Wesley's itinerant preachers and their families. The classes were led by a person chosen from the group who would work in association with the Methodist itinerant preachers and with Wesley in England or Asbury or other clergy in the United States.

In England, during those early decades, most of these class leaders were women. The class meetings allowed women a level of intellectual and spiritual equality not generally found in British society at the time. Women's thoughts and ideas were taken seriously. Women were affirmed for speaking about their own failings and victories. As they exhorted fellow group-members, prayed, and shared their testimonies, their voices moved into the public sphere. Their work with the sick and destitute brought recognition. Their involvement with decisions, planning, raising money, and in the finances of the societies spoke to an equality of the mind with men otherwise denied by the larger society, often even at home.

Grace Murray, Sarah Ryan, and Mary Bosanquet

Among the earliest Methodist leaders, the author includes Grace Murray who worked closely with Wesley in London and oversaw the Methodist classes in Newcastle. Sarah Ryan led Methodist work in Bristol and administered the Kingswood School. Later she would team up with Mary Bosanquet from Essex to create the first Methodist orphanage, Leytonstone, which also served as a school and hospital for the destitute. Though from opposite ends of the social-class spectrum, Sarah and Mary considered themselves soulmates. Together with a few other women, they would lead a semi-cloistered life of service that we find repeated often in Methodism, especially characteristic of the teaching and nursing missionaries of the late-nineteenth and early-twentieth centuries.

Barbara Heck

The introduction of Methodism into the colonies is often credited to Barbara Ruckle Heck who, with the help of a cousin, Philip Embury, organized the first formal Methodist society in New York. As the number of participants increased, they moved from Embury's living room to a rented hall and finally built a first Methodist meeting house, John Street Wesley Chapel, located in what today is the financial district of Manhattan.

Susanna Wesley

In retrospect, the class meetings that were fundamental to Methodism's first one hundred years were modeled on certain Sunday evening meetings that John and Charles's mother, Susanna Wesley, held when the two were boys. During the winter months of 1710–11 and 1711–12 when John Wesley's father, Samuel, spent long periods away from his Epworth parish, Susanna became concerned about the spiritual development of her children and expanded Sunday evening prayers with them and the house-servants to incorporate singing of Psalms and reading aloud a sermon from a book. Soon, neighbors and others from the parish began to attend also until the rectory was overflowing. Although the Church of England prohibited women from preaching and frowned on them publicly teaching men in the 1700s, John Wesley's father did not try to stop Susanna from these activities.

Methodism's First Authorized Woman Preacher, Sarah Crosby

Being Susanna's son, John Wesley was from the beginning more forward-thinking than most of his contemporaries. Still, his views about women's abilities to preach evolved over time. While a missionary in Georgia, he introduced the role of deaconesses into his ministry. In the 1740s in the Methodist societies, he expanded that role with Grace Murray and others to include much broader duties including ministering to the spiritual needs of men. And in the 1760s he acquiesced to a young woman's, Sarah Crosby's, calling to preach. In 1766, Sarah joined forces with Mary Bosanquet and Sarah Ryan at the Leytonstone orphanage and expanded her preaching from there.

Reaction and Repression

It is fair to say that Sarah Crosby, Mary Bosanquet (Fletcher), and many others forced open doors for women preachers. By the time Wesley died in March 1791, some of the more famous preachers in British Methodism were women. Perhaps the most famous was the evangelist Mary Barritt who was mentored into preaching by Wesley and was invited into the pulpits of many of the most respected preachers of British Methodism. But there was also a tide of opposition to the female preachers. And once Wesley died, the dike broke. The popularity of Mary Barritt and the other women preachers fostered jealousy. And there are some New Testament passages that can be interpreted as supporting only male preaching. Reactionaries at the 1802 Dublin Conference for Irish Methodism restricted the activities of women to the private sphere or only among other women. And a year later, the English Methodist preachers conferencing at Manchester followed suit, in large measure excluding women from Methodist pulpits for the next one hundred and sixty years.

Early America

Before separating from the Church of England, the foundational roles of women in Methodist class and band meetings were similar in America to those in England. We don't find women demanding the same right to preach, however. In America, the final break with the Anglican church occurred soon after the Revolutionary War ended, while Wesley was still alive. But when the Methodist Episcopal Church was created, at the Christmas Conference at Lovely Lane Chapel in Baltimore, Maryland, 1784, all the voting members were male and there was no discussion supporting women preachers. And the nineteenth century saw women's leadership in American Methodism further scaled back from colonial times to behind-the-scenes functions. Women were constricted into the private sphere of home and family where mothers were considered responsible for the moral education of their children and female sensibilities checked the immorality of husbands. Women's public leadership was largely confined to being role models—exemplars of self-giving love, silent strength, and humility.

Gopher Inclusion

The *Handbook*'s author uses the image of a gopher who tunnels underground but surfaces occasionally to describe the public leadership of women in American Methodism during the nineteenth and first half of the twentieth centuries. He mentions *Jarena Lee* (1783–1864) from Mother Bethel African Methodist Episcopal Church in Philadelphia who beginning in 1817 embarked on a fifty-year ministry as an evangelist; *Phoebe Worrell Palmer* (1807–74) who became the leading force of the holiness movement within the Methodist Episcopal Church; *Frances "Fanny" Jane Crosby* (1820–1915), American Methodism's most prolific hymn writer; and *Mary McLeod Bethune*, the educator, President of Bethune Cookman College, and force for civil rights who founded the National Council of Negro Women. But the author points out also that it was in foreign missions where Methodist women's public leadership came most to the fore and first returned to the near equality that existed in the class meetings of earliest Methodism. Although first going overseas as spouses, teachers, and nurses, the female missionaries' roles expanded to preachers, evangelizers, and organizers as evangelizing women and children often fell to them. Also, their involvement with education and nursing allowed the women missionaries closer access to native languages and customs and everyday people than the male preachers. And even when the views of the women missionaries originally limited their role to home and morality, the new setting forced them into activism as they opened schools, advocated for the rationality of girls, urged scientific medical treatment over magical incantations, and voiced opposition to such customs as foot-binding, concubinage, and arranged nuptials.

Women Clergy

Full clergy rights among Methodists came slowly and occurred first in the Methodist Protestant Church. It is generally thought that a circuit rider from Indiana, *Helenor Davisson*, in 1863 became American Methodism's first clergywoman. And of the next generation, the Reverend *Anna Howard Shaw* (1847–1919), who was denied ordination in the Methodist Episcopal Church, was ordained in 1880 when she transferred to the Methodist Protestant Church. Shaw would later earn a medical degree, become president of the National American Woman's Suffrage Association, and lecture throughout the United States and Europe for temperance, peace during World War I, and women's rights. In 1889, *Ella Niswonger* was ordained with full clergy rights in the American United Brethren Church that in 1968 joined the United Methodist Church. *Julia A. J. Foote* of the African Methodist Episcopal Zion Church was ordained a deacon in 1894 and elder in 1900. From the main body of Methodists, full clergy rights for women would only come in 1956 to a person who had been a missionary for forty-four years, *Maud Pauline Keister Jensen* (1904–98). The United Methodist Church elected its first female bishop, *Marjorie Matthews*, in 1980; the first female African American bishop, *Leontine T. Kelly*, in 1984; and the first openly lesbian bishop, *Karen Oliveto*, in 2016.

Where Do We Go from Here?

Have Methodists and like-minded Protestants in the United States reached gender equality? The author concludes the chapter by affirming that American Protestantism has progressed structurally in recognizing the historical contributions of women but that there is further to go before reaching the goal of spiritual and organizational equality in the church. He suggests that inclusiveness needs to manifest itself in institutional organization and provides several practical steps that can be taken by individuals and the church. Methodists and like-minded Christians should refuse to accommodate to prejudices and should consciously model Christian values for members and the larger community.

Terms, Dates, Events, and People

Define, identify, or explain each word and phrase as they appear in the *Handbook*'s chapter 9. Ask your instructor or look up words or phrases that remain unclear.

- Anne Hutchinson and Puritans
- Barbara Heck
- Christian nationalism
- Christmas Conference of 1784
- corporate guilt or societal guilt
- Evangelical United Brethren Church
- first and second wave feminism
- Frances Jane Crosby
- Francis Asbury
- itinerant preachers
- Jesus as an idol of rugged masculinity
- John Street Chapel
- Mary Bosanquet
- Mary Dyer
- Mary McLeod Bethune
- Methodist Protestant Church
- Nineteenth Amendment
- Sarah Crosby
- Sarah Ryan
- Seneca Falls Convention
- Susanna Wesley
- Thomas Coke
- women's movement

Reading Comprehension

Explain these important themes found in chapter 9. Discuss them with course partners. If the *Handbook for the Christian Faith*'s author were in the room with you, what questions would you ask? Can you think of further evidence to buttress the points the author makes?

1. Methodists and like-minded Christians hold inclusion essential to the church. All humans are children of God and brothers and sisters to

each other. Unfortunately, however, most churches have fallen short of establishing spiritual equality for men and women.

2. Courage and the affirmation of spiritual equality have been telltale marks of Quakers. Although many activists in the women's movement were motivated by sentiments intertwined with their faith, the women's movement itself did not spring from Christianity. In fact, some of the strongest opposition to women's equality has come from conservative Christian groups.

3. Women played an extensive role in the development of early Methodism. This included a strong leadership role.

4. In their eighteenth-century context, the class meetings of Methodism allowed women a level of intellectual and spiritual equality not generally found in British society at the time.

5. John Wesley placed Grace Murray, Sarah Ryan, and Mary Bosanquet in positions of responsibility and authority in eighteenth-century Methodism. Sarah Ryan administered Methodism's first school, Kingswood School, and later teamed up with Mary Bosanquet to create Methodism's first orphanage at Leytonstone. The orphanage also served as a school and hospital for the destitute.

6. Barbara Heck is credited by many with first bringing Methodism to America. Along with a cousin, Philip Embury, she helped organize the first formal Methodist society and later built the first Methodist meeting house in the colonies, John Street Wesley Chapel, in what today is Manhattan, New York.

7. In retrospect, the class meetings that were fundamental to early Methodism were modeled on certain Sunday evening meetings conducted by Suzanna Wesley when her sons, John and Charles, were young boys. In the 1700s, the Church of England prohibited women from preaching and teaching men. But Susanna expanded Sunday evening prayers with her children and house servants to include singing the psalms and reading a sermon. Others from the parish started attending, and soon more than two hundred were participating in the services in the rectory.

8. Wesley's views about women's abilities to preach evolved over time until in the 1760s he broke with the Church of England's prohibition against women preaching. He mentored Sarah Crosby, Sarah Ryan, Mary Bosanquet (Fletcher), Mary Barritt, and many others into a preaching ministry.

9. After Wesley died in March 1791, opposition to women's preaching gained strength in Methodism. Irish Methodism restricted the activities of women to the private sphere or only among other women in 1802; and English Methodism followed suit the next year. After the War of Independence and the 1784 Christmas Conference when Methodism first became a church separate from the Church of England, women's leadership and church activities in America were further scaled back to behind-the-scenes functions. And generally, women's roles were constricted into the private sphere of home and family.

10. In the nineteenth and first-half of the twentieth centuries, women's public leadership tunneled to the surface occasionally in American Methodism. The author provides examples. But it was in foreign missions where Methodist women began in earnest to recapture the shared-leadership role that had been common during Wesley's day.

11. A Methodist woman first reached clergy status in 1863 in the Methodist Protestant Church. In the main Methodist denomination, it would only be in 1956 that the missionary Maud Pauline Keister Jensen was granted full clergy rights.

12. Although American Protestantism has progressed structurally in recognizing the historical contributions of women, the *Handbook*'s author urges that more work lies ahead if Methodists and like-minded Christians are to reach the ideal that once baptized, there are neither male nor female, for all are one in Christ (Gal 3:28).

Exercises to Enhance Understanding

1. In pairs or as a group, read the following two biblical passages: Galatians 3:27–28 and 1 Corinthians 14:34–35. Share your thoughts on these contradictory passages that relate to the role of women in the Christian church. In what ways does your own church emphasize one or the other of these two perspectives? What are possible ways for these passages to be in conversation with one another?

2. The author discusses numerous examples of women who were "ahead of their time" in terms of their leadership in the early church, including some who served as preachers and teachers. From these examples, choose one woman whose story resonated with you. Discuss your choice in pairs or in a small group. Why was this particular story compelling for you?

3. Initiate a conversation with a woman in ministry. What difficulties or roadblocks has she faced because of her gender? What stories did she share of affirmation from church members or colleagues who have provided encouragement to her?

Suggested Readings

From the Bible: The book of Ruth; Romans 16.

Baker, Jean H. *Sisters: The Lives of America's Suffragists*. New York: Hill and Wang, 2005.

Chilcote, Paul Wesley. *She Offered Them Christ: The Legacy of Women Preachers in Early Methodism*. Nashville: Abingdon, 1993.

Dallimore, Arnold A. *Susanna Wesley: The Mother of John and Charles Wesley*. Grand Rapids: Baker, 1993.

Fell, Margaret. "'Women's Speaking Justified, Proved, and Allowed of By the Scriptures. All Such as Speak By the Spirit and Power of the Lord Jesus' (ca. 1666–16667)." *Quaker Heritage Press*, July 7, 2013. http://www.qhpress.org/texts/fell.html.

Murdock, Norman H. "Female Ministry in the Thought and Work of Catherine Booth." *Church History* 53.3 (September 1984) 348–62.

Palmer, Phoebe. *Promise of the Father: Or, A Neglected Specialty of the Last Days, Addressed to the Clergy and Laity of All Christian Communities*. Eugene, OR: Wipf and Stock, 2015.

Whitlow, William H. *Barbara Heck: A Tale of Early Methodism*. Toronto: Methodist Mission Rooms, 1895. https://archive.org/details/barbarahecktaleoowithuoft/page/1/mode/2up.

10

The Ideal of Equality and History of Racism

Overview and Summary of Content

CHAPTER 10 OF THE *Handbook for the Christian Faith* opens by recalling reactions to the congressman Reverend John Lewis's death in the summer of 2020. Lewis had been a companion of Dr. Martin Luther King Jr. and was an icon of the civil rights movement of the 1960s. And following his passing, many people celebrated his life and accomplishments. But not all celebrated. For American society remains deeply divided on the matter of race. In the words of the author, "When it comes to race, the United States [remains] a nation of contradictions and dissonance." And although the divide is more covert than as existed when Lewis was a young man, it is still very much present when examining statistical evidence concerning incarceration, poverty, etc. In a sense, our nation's racialization is hidden in plain sight. And it is present in Christian churches too.

America's Original Sin

Though not often mentioned in our history books, slavery arrived in Virginia more than a full year before the Pilgrims disembarked from the *Mayflower*. Unfortunately, it walked hand-in-hand with Christianity throughout the colonial period and our nation's early history. Some of America's most revered Christian leaders defended slavery and owned slaves. These included Roger Williams (1603–83); Cotton Mather (1663–1738); Jonathan Edwards (1703–58); and the great English evangelist and companion of the Wesley brothers in the Holy Club, George Whitefield (1714–70), whose sermons along with those of Jonathan Edwards and Gilbert Tennent were most responsible for the Great Awakening and implanting evangelicalism in America.

The Methodist Abolitionist Impulse

John Wesley's difference with these slavery-supporting divines was sharp. His *Thoughts on Slavery* was a widely circulated abolitionist writing that helped end chattel slavery on the British mainland. And the last letter Wesley penned was to fellow Anglican evangelical William Wilberforce (1759–1833), encouraging him to continue to fight in Parliament to outlaw the enslavement of Africans, not just on the mainland but everywhere in the British Empire. And on this side of the Atlantic, the founding Christmas Conference of American Methodism in 1784 adopted a measure to expel from the new church all and any who would not emancipate their slaves. The first bishops of American Methodism, Thomas Coke and Francis Asbury, so opposed slavery as to endanger their own lives and went so far as to ask George Washington personally on the part of the Methodists that the new nation take up and pass a Methodist petition to emancipate slaves.

About half of the first Methodist congregation at John Street Chapel were African descendants, some free and some slaves. And there were sizable congregations of Blacks in Philadelphia, Baltimore, Charleston, and other cities. The author provides statistics showing that 20–30 percent of Methodist society members during that early period were African Americans. And the author recounts also some of the documented accomplishments of the early African American Methodists, mentioning the preaching of Harry Hosier and his participation in the Christmas Conference where Methodism became a distinct denomination and the ministry of John Stewart who is credited with being American Methodism's first missionary.

Accommodation to Slavery

So, what happened to Wesley's and Methodism's early impulse toward racial equality, the author asks? Accommodation to American slavery started early and was partly responsible in 1794 for the first schism in the newly formed Methodist Episcopal Church. The first discipline of the new denomination that promised excommunication for participating in slavery was never enforced, and by 1804 Methodists were publishing two Books of Discipline, one for slaveholding states that was no longer demanding laypeople divest themselves of slaves.

In retrospect, Methodism's accommodation to the economy and culture of slavery proved stronger than the religion's stated ideals and its own rules. Many in the new church, even among those who opposed the institution of slavery, thought of Whites as being intellectually and morally superior to Blacks. And then, too, there was the extreme privatization of religion that was present in evangelicalism from its inception but intensified in the Southern slaveholding states. White Methodists in the slave society became comfortable applying religion strictly to their spiritual relationship with Christ, separating loving Christ from loving Black neighbors. Until finally in 1836, the Methodist Episcopal Church passed a resolution at General Conference opposing ministerial agitation toward abolition and promising to put any that arose down.

The Emergence of the African Methodist Episcopal (AME) Church and the African Methodist Episcopal Zion (AMEZ) Church

Former slave Richard Allen (1760–1831) participated along with Harry Hosier in the 1784 Christmas Conference and was dedicated to Methodism. But already prior to the founding conference, while ministering in Philadelphia, a problem broke out when Whites insisted on segregated pews for worship. In protest, Allen had led a small group of Blacks to leave the St. George Methodist Episcopal Church and form the Bethel Methodist Episcopal Church (1773). But never quite able to escape White oversight, Allen and Bethel broke denominational ties in 1816, becoming the foundational congregation of the African Methodist Episcopal (AME) Church. A year later, approximately two thousand Black Methodists followed in leaving the Methodist Episcopal Church in Charleston, South Carolina, and joining the AME Church as Mother Emanuel Church. The main issue leading to the exodus had been a White decision ignoring Black protestations to build a carriage house on top of a Black cemetery.

A similar separation over church polity and the voice of Blacks in church governance led to the founding of the African Methodist Episcopal Zion Church. In the 1790s, the Black members of John Street Methodist Church in New York began to worship separate from the White congregants on Sunday afternoons, building their own place of worship, in 1799–1800. The church was incorporated such that all trustees must be African descendants. There were discussions about joining Allen's AME emerging denomination, but in 1820–21 the New York congregation followed its own course under the leadership of *Bishop James Varick*.

Separation and Control

After the 1836 General Conference's resolution threatening ministers who agitated for the end of slavery, most White Methodist preachers in Southern states like Virginia, even those who were sympathetic to the cause, stopped preaching abolition. Blacks understood the betrayal of earlier Wesleyan ideals of brotherhood and sought settings where they could speak openly about the evils of slavery. And there were also other issues of racial insensitivity affecting matters of worship and polity that led Blacks to seek their own places of worship. Yet, the drive to separate also brought its own anxieties to Whites as they still wished to oversee the development of Black Christianity. And there was a persistent fear of slave revolts driving Southern Whites to maintain control in their own hands.

In partial response, Southern Methodists, Baptists, and Presbyterians in the 1830s and 1840s threw tremendous effort into home missions for Blacks. The White missionaries to the Southern plantations preached the Creator's design of an orderly society, the virtue of suffering, respect of authority, and the promise of a reward in heaven. And not just Southerners and not just Whites, but many Northerners and Blacks furthered efforts of The American Colonization Society, founded in 1816, to repatriate freedmen to the west coast of Africa.

Division, Segregation, and Southern Civil Protestantism

While Methodists in the free states remained organizationally true to Wesley's abhorrence of slavery, most antebellum Southern preachers and their parishioners affirmed a type of Christian White supremacy. The Methodist Episcopal Church's split over slavery was inevitable and occurred in a formal way in the 1840s when the slave owner from Georgia, James Osgood Andrew, was selected as a bishop. The new Methodist Episcopal Church, South denomination was formed at a specially called convention in Louisville, Kentucky, in May 1845.

The victory of the Union in the Civil War and passage of the Thirteenth Amendment in 1865 ended slavery but did not heal the separation. Reconstruction and the suffering of the South turned Southern Christianity even more toward personal piety and away from social reform than before the war, and it reemphasized the otherworldliness of Christianity, leading to further separation in worship between Whites and Blacks. The CME (formerly Colored Methodist Episcopal, today Christian Methodist Episcopal) Church was formed in 1866–70 when the General Conference of the

Methodist Episcopal Church, South, decided that it was in the interest of both Whites and Blacks to separate both for worship and organizationally.

Among White Southern Christians in general, the lost war morphed into a Lost Cause where symbols of battle flag and heroic statues took on quasi-religious meaning. Pietism took the form of good or cultured manners with emphasis on prayer in publicly visible moments. Bible interpretation became even more spiritualized and more personalized than it had been before the war; the focus on evangelism shifted away from the Blacks and Native Americans to distant lands. In the segregated Protestantism of the South, White supremacy continued unabated with Black servants replacing household slaves and Black tenant farmers replacing plantation slaves.

The Road to Reunification

The path toward greater racial equality has been painfully slow and, as with movement toward women's equality, grew from the mission field. When Methodist and like-minded Protestant missionaries would return to the United States and visit Southern congregations to raise support for evangelism, churches, schools, orphanages, care facilities, hospitals, leprosy asylums, etc., they brought back their stories and photographs of their mixed congregations, of believers with different hues of skin worshiping and working side by side. Formal first steps toward racial reconciliation happened in 1939 at a specially called reunification General Conference when the Methodist Episcopal Church, the Methodist Episcopal Church, South, and the Methodist Protestant Church reunited into the Methodist Church. And it continued in 1968 when the Evangelical United Brethren Church and the Methodist Church joined to form the United Methodist Church. Although continuing as separate denominations, the United Methodist Church, the African Methodist Episcopal Church, the African Methodist Episcopal Zion Church, and the Christian Methodist Episcopal Church in 2012 joined in the sense that they agreed to affirm each other's clergy, ministries, and Wesleyan heritage.

The Deeper Path toward Reconciliation

The *Handbook*'s author concludes his historical survey of the racial division that has scarred American Methodists and like-minded Christians by recalling a four-point plan for reconciliation that emerged during the civil rights era. The steps of developing intimate friendships and worshiping together, recognizing and resisting unjust social structures, urging Whites to repent and Blacks to forgive and let go of anger are excellent but undercount, in the author's view, the suffering necessary to overcome hate.

Where Do We Go from Here?

The author concludes the chapter by urging that Christians commit themselves to changing the damning statistics that show the racial divide in our nation and churches. The commitment includes acknowledging and confessing individual and group failings and leaving our comfort zones.

Terms, Dates, Events, and People

Define, identify, or explain each word and phrase as they appear in the *Handbook*'s chapter 10. Ask your instructor or look up words or phrases that remain unclear.

- African Methodist Episcopal Church and African Methodist Episcopal Zion Church
- American Colonization Society and repatriation
- American Missionary Association
- America's original sin
- Bloody Sunday, 1965
- Central Jurisdiction
- church polity
- civil religion and Southern White civil Protestantism
- Frederick Douglass
- freedom riders
- General Board of Global Ministries
- George Whitefield
- institutional racism
- Lost Cause
- Bishop John Emory
- Methodist Church in Brazil
- private sin

- *satyagraha* or "love in action"
- Southern Christian Leadership Conference
- White supremacy

Reading Comprehension

Explain these important themes found in chapter 10. Discuss them with course partners. If the *Handbook for the Christian Faith*'s author were in the room with you, what questions would you ask? Can you think of further evidence to buttress the points the author makes?

1. When it comes to race, the United States is a nation of contradictions and dissonance. The racial divide is not what existed before the passage of the 1964 Civil Rights Act and other congressional legislation but continues to exist.

2. Racialization in our nation is more covert than sixty years ago. But it is clearly visible in statistics showing incarceration and poverty rates. While some people credit current racialization only to vestiges of the past and to individual prejudice and ignorance, the *Handbook*'s author holds that racism continues to stretch its tentacles into the structures of society.

3. Slavery arrived in colonial America before the pilgrims disembarked from the *Mayflower*. Some of the venerated religious figures of colonial America supported slavery and were White supremacists.

4. John Wesley and early Methodists opposed slavery and worked to abolish it. The founding organizational meeting of American Methodism in 1784 adopted a measure to expel from the new church all and any who would not emancipate their slaves.

5. Many accomplishments of early Black Methodists have not been fully recognized by Whites or have been forgotten completely. An exception is the Black man John Stewart who is remembered and credited with being American Methodism's first missionary.

6. By the beginning of the nineteenth century, Methodists were accommodating to slavery in the slave states. In the South, the economy and culture of slavery proved stronger than the religion's stated ideals and its own rules.

7. The African Methodist Episcopal Church and the African Methodist Episcopal Zion Church became separate denominations from the Methodist Episcopal Church in the early nineteenth century. The division occurred not because of doctrinal differences but because of racial insensitivity on the part of Whites in matters of worship and over church polity, especially the voice of Blacks in church governance.

8. Partly out of fear of slave revolts, Southern Whites were keen to oversee the development of Black Christianity. They placed effort into home missions for Blacks. Whites also supported efforts to repatriate freedmen to the west coast of Africa.

9. Tensions over slavery led the Methodist Episcopal Church to split in the 1840s. But the victory of the Union in the Civil War and the passage of constitutional amendments ending slavery did not lead Southern Christians to repentance. Rather, Southern religion continued to hold itself a purer Christianity than found in the North.

10. A Southern White civil Protestantism emerged in the second half of the nineteenth century and first half of the twentieth century where pietism took the form of cultured manners and prayer in publicly visible moments. Bible interpretation became even more spiritualized and personalized than it had been before the war. White supremacy continued.

11. American Methodism's greater acceptance and empowerment of Blacks occurred slowly. Among Whites, it began on the mission field with formal changes occurring with the reunification General Conferences of 1939 and 1968. It is the author's view that there is much more to do, however. In local congregations, work includes a greater commitment to change, a willingness to leave comfort zones behind, and taking concrete steps to recreate church worship.

Exercises to Enhance Understanding

1. In pairs or as a group, discuss the author's statement that "when it comes to race, the United States is a nation of contradictions and dissonance." How can practices of individual and corporate confession and reconciliation address the sin of racism? Share specific examples. What should be the role of the Christian church in terms of creating ways to make space and opportunity for confession and reconciliation?

2. As a denomination, the contemporary United Methodist Church has entered another significant period of disunity and separation because of opposing views related to human sexuality. Do you recognize any parallels between the issue of race in early American Methodism and the issues the denomination faces today? In what ways has your own congregation been impacted by these issues and related events of separation from both past and present?

3. Many historic, mainline Protestant churches remain mostly segregated by race today as a matter of either tradition or choice even though racial segregation is no longer codified by law in our society. Why do you think this is so? What reasons related to worship, traditions, or underlying systemic issues might this be attributed to? In pairs or in a group, discuss the role issues of race in the church have played in your own community and congregation.

4. Consider the programs and missions of your own church. Which of these are specifically about working for social justice? Is social justice a phrase that is ignored or avoided in your congregation? If so, why? Do you think Christians tend to focus more narrowly on "spiritual matters" as a way of avoiding controversial social issues and matters of social justice? How central is social justice to the message of the gospel?

Suggested Readings

Douglass, Frederick. *The Portable Frederick Douglass*. Edited by John Stauffer and Henry Louis Gates Jr. New York: Penguin, 2016.

Emerson, Michael O., and Christian Smith. *Divided by Faith: Evangelical Religion and the Problem of Race in America*. Oxford: Oxford University Press, 2000.

Irons, Charles F. *The Origins of Proslavery Christianity: White and Black Evangelicals in Colonial and Antebellum Virginia*. Chapel Hill: The University of North Carolina Press, 2008.

Jones, Robert P. *White Too Long: The Legacy of White Supremacy in American Christianity*. New York: Simon & Schuster, 2020.

King, Martin Luther, Jr. "The Current Crisis in Race Relations (1958)." In *A Testament of Hope: The Essential Writings and Speeches of Martin Luther King, Jr.*, edited by James Melvin Washington, 85–90. New York: Harper Collins, 1991.

———. "Letter from Birmingham City Jail (1963)." In *A Testament of Hope: The Essential Writings and Speeches of Martin Luther King, Jr.*, edited by James Melvin Washington, 289–302. New York: Harper Collins, 1991.

Meacham, Jon. *His Truth Is Marching On: John Lewis and the Power of Hope*. New York: Random, 2020.

Newman, Richard E. *Freedom's Prophet: Bishop Richard Allen, the AME Church, and the Black Founding Fathers*. New York: New York University Press, 2009.

Shockley, Grant S. "The A.M.E. and A.M.E. Zion Churches." In vol. 2 of *History of American Methodism*, edited Emory Steven Bucke, 526–84. Nashville: Abingdon, 1964.

Wesley, John. *Thoughts upon Slavery*. 1773. Reprint, Philadelphia: Joseph Crukshank, 1778.

11

The LGBTQ+ Community

Overview and Summary of Content

THE *HANDBOOK*'S AUTHOR WROTE chapter 11 during the months that the United Methodist Church was confronting imminent schism. At the time, discussion was ongoing concerning principally two related issues: whether to sanction the marriage of LGBTQ+ couples and whether to ordain practicing homosexuals. Those opposed to full acceptance were contemplating parting ways to form a separate community of faith to be called the Global Methodist Church.

Methodists and other Christians have historically proscribed homosexual acts as sinful—and prior to 1962, sodomy was a felony in every state. As recently as 1952, the American Psychiatric Association's diagnostic manual listed homosexuality as a sociopathic personality disturbance. But there has been a sea change in the last fifty years concerning what American society deems normative sexual behavior. And although not thinking that church practice and doctrine should be governed by culture, the author hoped that the church would avoid the coming division and take the path of inclusion already coursed by American Episcopalians and the Presbyterian Church USA. This chapter presents his reasons.

Do No Harm

The author opens his argument by reminding us that the first rule for participating in the early Methodist class meetings was to do no harm. And the principal reason he is saddened by the division that is taking place in the United Methodist Church is the amount of hurt engendered. He then offers personal examples of the pain experienced as our country's mores have changed in the last half-century. Although some Methodists were looking forward to separation as a new beginning, the author suggests that the division will not lessen the suffering but rather add to it and asks, "How can the church be an instrument of reconciliation for the world if it is not reconciled with itself?"

The Primacy of the Biblical Argument?

Traditionalists cite several arguments against the full acceptance of LGBTQ+ people into the community of believers. These include the church's historical practices; the supposed influence that the LGBTQ+ leaders might exert on susceptible church members, especially the young; and the idea that the purpose of sex is to have children, and children are best nurtured in families with a loving father and mother modeling Christian values.

But it is a fourth argument that traditionalists claim determinative. True to Methodism's evangelical roots, traditionalists tend to hinge the exclusion of LGBTQ+ Christians from full fellowship on the authority of Scripture. Traditionalists have culled certain passages from the Bible, which they often use as proof texts. By the author's count, their scriptural argument rests on just nine—Genesis 2:21–25; Genesis 19:1–14; Leviticus 18:22; Leviticus 20:13; Romans 1:26–27; 1 Corinthians 6:9; 1 Timothy 1:10; 2 Peter 2:6–8; and Jude 7. After enumerating the passages, the author promises to discuss each individually, with two overarching questions in mind: Have the traditionalists correctly interpreted these passages? And are these few passages enough to bear the weight of church division being laid upon them?

Preliminary Considerations

But before examining those passages, the *Handbook*'s author urges caution. He asks that we remember that bad actors have often misused the Bible by taking passages out of context to support cruelty, injustice, and abuse of many kinds. Furthermore, the Bible speaks on many subjects that American churchgoers think of as time or culturally conditioned and thus disregard. Also, he points out that having listed the passages featured in discussions about homosexuality, there is relatively little in the Bible about the topic with Jesus and the Hebrew prophets saying nothing about the subject. And finally, he reminds us that the Bible is clear, however, about other sexual prescriptions, many of which Americans disregard.

Featured Biblical Passages

Tabling the question of why Christians might choose to emphasize some passages in the Bible while deeming others as culturally and historically conditioned, the author then carefully examines each of the passages identified as foundational for the traditionalist argument for not including LGBTQ+ persons fully into Christian fellowship. His analysis places the passages in their historical and literary contexts and attempts to draw out their meaning as intended at the time of composition. He finds that because of our distance in time and place from ancient Israel and the Mediterranean world of first century Christianity, the meanings of the passages are not always clear to us today. It is obvious, however, that none of the passages speak directly about the church's present-day concerns with the ordination of ministers and ministers officiating marriages between consenting male and female same-sex partners who wish to express mutual feelings and commitment to each other before God and a community of friends.

The concept of sexual orientation held by modern society is alien to the Bible, and the passages betray cultural mores and practices regarding slavery, pederasty, pagan worship, imitative magic, and other issues quite distant from the American experience today. There are issues of Baal and Asherah worship featured in several passages important to their original intent that are overlooked by the modern discussion. And then there are other issues of interpretation. God's creation of two beings from the androgenous Adam in Genesis, for instance, seems to have as much to do with companionship as with the procreation and nurture of children. And the Sodom story seems less about homosexual passion and more about rape, power, and xenophobia than traditionalists allow.

Conclusions?

The author refuses to disparage either LGBTQ+ Christians or the traditionalists (that is, those United Methodists who soon broke away to form the Global Methodist Church). After reiterating the central role played by the biblical discussion within the Methodist community, he concludes that proponents for separation are mistaken when claiming that the Bible speaks with a clear voice in opposition to the ordination of self-avowed, practicing homosexuals and against the union of committed homosexual couples. The Bible says little that even tangentially touches upon these topics. And while Paul, steeped in the teachings and customs of his people, would have almost certainly opposed same-sex unions, the Romans 1:26–27 and 1 Corinthians

6:9 passages often cited in discussion hardly fit our modern situation where people of the same sex wish before God and community to commit themselves to love and be faithful each to the other for life. The Leviticus and other Old Testament passages inform us about what the Hebrew priests who wrote those writings 3,000–2,400 years ago thought. But what exactly did they think? Somehow, the author urges, twenty-first-century Christians must be honest enough to accept that these nine passages say little about our modern situation concerning homosexual ordination and marriage.

So, to the question, can the church be sure enough about the traditionalist interpretation of the Scriptures to exclude the LGBTQ+ community from full fellowship in the church, the answer must be No! And as for the seriousness of the decision about separation: Are these few passages enough to bear the weight of denominational schism being laid upon them? And again, the author answers No!

Stories

The author finishes the chapter by moving away from a historical-critical discussion of Scripture to stories about people. Principal among Methodists and like-minded Christians are the demands of love. And stories provide perspective. The stories chosen and retold by the author illustrate the themes of God's suffering love and his willingness to encounter us in unexpected ways.

Placing the legalistic discussion of Scripture aside, in the closing pages of the chapter the author returns to a key Wesleyan and Reformation view of the Bible. Twenty-first-century American Christians should eschew literalism in favor of recapturing the spirit of Scripture. And according to the spirit of Scripture love should take precedence in the church (and in society). As the author concludes, it is deep wisdom that grandmothers are going to love their grandbabies. Love is God's way. And it applies as much to LGBTQ+ grandbabies as to others.

Where Do We Go from Here?

The author suggests that today's United Methodists could learn better how to live with ambiguity. What Wesley learned after Aldersgate and early Methodists learned as they searched for holiness in their class meetings was that discipleship and loving others were more significant than any feeling of certainty. All could benefit from placing less emphasis on doctrinal integrity and giving more attention to being responsible for the claims of Christian love. And finally, in situations where sides must be taken, Christians should remember that solidarity must always be with those suffering injustice. Being church means being a family of God.

Terms, Dates, Events, and People

Define, identify, or explain each word and phrase as they appear in the *Handbook*'s chapter 11. Ask your instructor or look up words or phrases that remain unclear.

- Asherah
- Baal and *baal*
- do no harm rule for Methodist class meetings
- the Global Methodist Church
- grace through separation
- *Ish/Ishah*
- Justinian's Novella 77
- Leviticus Holiness Code
- Molech
- pederastic relationships
- prooftext
- Protocol of Reconciliation
- time or culturally conditioned
- xenophobia
- *yada*

Reading Comprehension

Explain these important themes found in chapter 11. Discuss them with course partners. If the *Handbook for the Christian Faith*'s author were in the room with you, what questions would you ask? Can you think of further evidence to buttress the points the author makes?

1. The *Handbook for the Christian Faith* was written during the time that the United Methodist Church was on the verge of dividing over issues

of same-sex marriage: Should the denomination ordain practicing homosexuals? Should United Methodist ministers be allowed to perform same-sex marriages? Should church facilities and funds be liberalized to support LGBTQ+ concerns? The author argued against the coming schism.

2. Historically, Christianity has proscribed homosexual acts as sinful. If not heterosexual, celibacy was considered an acceptable option. But in the last fifty years, there has been a sea change with regards to LGBTQ+ rights and what Americans consider normative sexual behavior. Much of the change has been driven by new scientific understandings of human sexuality.

3. The first rule for participating in the early Methodist class meetings was to do no harm. And the principal reason that the *Handbook*'s author claims to be saddened by the division taking place is the unnecessary hurt engendered. "How can the church be an instrument of reconciliation for the world if it is not reconciled with itself?" the author asks.

4. Although traditionalists cite several arguments against the full inclusion of LGBTQ+ people in the community of believers, they most stress biblical reasons. They refer to a number of specific texts when making their argument, nine by the author's count.

5. Before considering the particular passages most featured in discussion, the author cautions that the Bible has often been misused; that it speaks on many subjects that twenty-first-century readers think of as time and culturally conditioned and thus disregard; that the ancient writings have relatively little to say that touches on same-sex marriage; and that the Bible is clear about other sexual prescriptions that Americans, including Methodists, completely disregard.

6. Traditionalists argue that Genesis establishes the family paradigm for society with males and females joining for the purpose of birthing and nurturing children. But the concept of companionship is strong in Genesis as God states his motivation with the creation of woman in Genesis 2:18: "It is not good that Adam should be alone; I will make for him a helper and a partner."

7. Many traditionalists hold that the sin leading to the destruction of Sodom in the Genesis account is homosexuality. But the story of the attempted rape and violence against outsiders, God's messengers, has little to say about the ordination of homosexual ministers or about ministers officiating marriages between same-sex partners who wish

to express mutual feelings and commitment to each other before God and a community of faith.

8. There are some Bible passages that at face value prohibit same-sex relations. But the meaning of the passages is not clear. Some might be prohibitions against idolatry instead of homosexuality, for Canaanite worship included sexual activity. And in the New Testament, some of the statements might be prohibitions against pederasty, male prostitution, or pedophilia instead of consenting same-sex relations.

9. It is the author's view that the proponents for separation are mistaken when claiming that the Bible speaks with a strong and clear voice in opposition to the ordination of self-avowed, practicing homosexuals, and against the union of committed homosexual couples. The Bible says little that even tangentially touches upon these topics. And Christians should have the humility and courage to admit as much.

10. Legalistic uses of biblical texts to exclude people who are sexually different from full fellowship with the community of faith should give way to the demands of Christian love. The spirit of Scripture shows that God meets us in unexpected ways and that Christian love should take precedence over doctrinal integrity in the church.

11. Christian solidarity must always be with those suffering injustice.

Exercises to Enhance Understanding

1. Consider some of the changes to public opinion and perceptions regarding social norms or issues that have taken place over your own lifetime. For example, general perceptions of interracial marriage have changed significantly in the last few decades. In what ways might it be said that the Christian church most often, if not always, lags behind the tide of public opinion on many social issues? In what ways might the Christian church be perceived by society at large as being a place where people are not accepted or welcomed because of matters of identity? Are there any specific ways your own congregation works to cultivate and communicate a spirit of welcome or openness in the community?

2. Revisit the author's discussion of nine proof texts used to exclude LGBTQ+ Christians from full fellowship in the church (235–43). In pairs or as a small group, share one or two in particular that stood

out to you. What did you find compelling or surprising? What questions were raised that you had not considered before? What are your thoughts on the idea of individual biblical passages that seem contradictory to the whole counsel of Scripture and the story of God's love woven into humanity?

3. In what ways has your own congregation been impacted by the issues related to LGBTQ+ Christians and the subsequent disunion taking place in the United Methodist Church? Where does your own church find itself at this polarizing moment related to questions of human sexuality? Have views and opinions changed in any way? In what ways do you think this issue affects the perception of the Christian church by those who do not attend or belong to a church?

Suggested Readings

Baber, Charles. *Incompatible: How the Church Cast Out LGBTQ Christians & Where We Go Next*. Eugene, OR: Cascade, 2023.

Cantrell, Robert Wil. *Unafraid and Unashamed: Facing the Future of United Methodism*. Knoxville: Market Square, 2017.

Creech, Jimmy. *Adam's Gift: A Memoir of a Pastor's Calling to Defy the Church's Persecution of Lesbians and Gays*. Durham: Duke University Press, 2011.

Edwards, George. *Gay & Lesbian Liberation: A Biblical Perspective*. Louisville: John Knox, 1991.

Martinson, Roland D. "Sexual Orientation: The History and Significance of an Idea." *Word & World* 14.3 (Summer 1994) 239–45.

Ratzinger, Joseph Cardinal. "Considerations Regarding Proposals to Give Legal Recognition to Unions between Homosexual Persons." Congregation for the Doctrine of the Faith, June 3, 2003. https://www.vatican.va/roman_curia/congregations/cfaith/documents/rc_con_cfaith_doc_20030731_homosexual-unions_en.html.

Rosner, Brian. "Temple Prostitution in I Corinthians 6:12–20," *Novum Testamentum*, 40.4 (October 1998) 336–51.

Wilde, Oscar, "The Happy Prince." Oscar Wilde Online, 2007. https://www.wilde-online.info/the-happy-prince.html.

12

Evangelism and the Great Awakening

Overview and Summary of Content

PART V OF THE *Handbook for the Christian Faith* concerns the nature and task of the church. The author begins chapter 12 by recalling the book of Acts' description of early Christianity's rapid growth. By the end of the first generation, the religion had spread from Jerusalem to Rome and increased in numbers by many thousands.

Evangelism

Evangelism is simply bringing God's good news to people mired in bad situations. It is what Jesus did, it was what the apostles did, and it was what John Wesley and Francis Asbury did. Sometimes these Methodist founders preached to massive crowds, but more often they spoke to modest groups of listeners. Very active in spreading the gospel were also early Methodist lay preachers who reported directly to Wesley in Great Britain or a bishop in the United States after 1784, traveled assigned circuits, and oversaw the work of the Methodist societies. Their preaching was religious, moral, and egalitarian, as much concerned for the souls of housemaids as for leaders of society. The author adds that it would be a mistake to confuse Wesley's dry, written sermons intended for publication with Methodism's oral preaching. Wesleyan Methodism was socially leveling.

The first itinerants in America were on average young and single. They were devoted to spreading the gospel, and the church grew quickly. American Methodism increased from a membership of 1,160 with only lay preachers in 1773, to 14,988 and a baker's dozen ordained ministers in 1784, to over 200,000 members and over 700 ordained clergy the year Asbury died in 1816. By 1820, American Methodism reported 259,890 church members. The *Handbook*'s author points out that these figures rival the spread of Christianity reported in the Book of Acts.

Medicine for Your Soul

The author pulls an example from the mission field to help us today visualize the dedication to spreading the gospel that carried those early Methodist preachers forward and the accompanying leveling of society brought about by their preaching. He describes a lay preacher, Manoel de Paula, traveling his circuit in the 1970s in the interior of South America in the region bordering Brazil and Paraguay. De Paula had no parsonage to live in and would travel from one place to another—sleeping, eating, and preaching in the homes of the scattered members. After staying a week or so in a particular place and baptizing, marrying, instructing and receiving members, and preaching, he would go somewhere else. People would come on horseback or on foot or by boat from miles around to hear his simple sermons. Holy communion was offered after preaching with bread broken from a loaf and a spoonful of wine from a bottle as "medicine for your soul."

Awakening and Evangelism in the Wesleyan Spirit

As mentioned, American Methodism initially experienced rapid growth such that by the beginning of the twentieth century its membership was comparable to what it is today. Then, it stopped growing. So, what happened?

In the 1971 Denman Lectureship in Evangelism, the Methodist scholar Albert Outler pointed out that Methodism became a vibrant movement not at the time of Wesley's Aldersgate experience when his heart was strangely warmed but when his passion turned to compassion—that is when in April 1739 Wesley's focus changed foremost toward the needs of others. Instead of focusing on the assurance of his own salvation, Wesley became compassionate for other people's salvation, their well-being, and their need to experience the good news of God's grace. Outler pointed out, second, that for Wesley and the early Methodists, the conversion experience was never more than the starting point of evangelism. Beyond confessing Christ as Lord and Savior, early Methodists were converted toward a new way of living. Third, Outler indicated that Wesley and the first Methodists balanced that inner experience of faith with the expectation of public and social evidence for faith. Methodists were expected to do no harm, do good, and keep the ordinances of the faith. And fourth, Methodism grew through the witness and the work of laypeople. Outler noted that beyond the essential efforts of the lay preachers, the witness of society members sharing their experiences in class meetings and through everyday contact proved especially powerful in spreading the gospel. Women and men were evangelized by being attracted to the Christian lives of people they knew.

George Whitefield's Competing Evangelism

One of John and Charles Wesley's companions while at Oxford was George Whitefield, who would become a famous evangelist in both Great Britain and colonial America. He was a member of the Holy Club, ordained in the Church of England, and he would follow the Wesley brothers to America. In Georgia he founded our nation's oldest childcare institution, Bethesda Orphan House and Academy. Whitefield had a charismatic personality and was a powerful speaker. And along with Jonathan Edwards and George Tennent, Whitefield is remembered for leading a religious movement that church historians refer to as the First Great Awakening.

Whitefield was well-known for preaching outdoors in city squares, parks, fields, wherever people gathered. Huge crowds came to hear him. He had a flair for the dramatic and preached to convict his hearers. His sermons combined theatrics, emotional appeal, and often some measure of patriotism. They were filled with anecdotes, imitation, humor, pathos. He tended to stress feelings, and he emphasized the necessity, regardless of baptism, for everyone to experience a new birth in Christ. His goal was to awaken the spiritual passions among the elect and create enthusiasm for Christianity.

Parting of the Ways

The *Handbook*'s author sees in Whitefield the genesis of the attractions and weaknesses of modern-day evangelicalism. There were the crowds, the excitement for religion, the stirring of the spirit, the child-like faith in the Bible, the mixing together of Christianity and nationalism; but also, the emotionalism, the attack on reason, the naïve approach to Scripture, the insistence on tangential doctrines that led to incessant infighting and division. He emphasized personal salvation and was much less interested than Wesley in the welfare of the community of faith.

Although having drawn close at Oxford, Whitefield's and John Wesley's friendship was difficult. In their dedication to evangelizing and to living a holy life, the two were cut from the same bolt. But they had a falling out over doctrine and slavery. When in America Whitefield became an owner of slaves and a stalwart supporter of the institution of slavery, something

Wesley considered despicable. Also, Whitefield emphasized election. God so fully controlled history, Whitefield thought, that God selected some people to be saved while damning the rest of humanity. But Wesley preached that Christ died for everyone. God wished for all to respond to Jesus' knocking at the door. There was still time. Though justified by the grace of God, people nevertheless had choice in their own salvation. And they might lose salvation, too, if careless. Whitefield emphasized the altar call moment, an event laden with emotion and known through feeling. But, despite his own heart-warming experience, Wesley hesitated to give so much attention to one moment in a lifetime of moments. He insisted on preceding or prevenient grace. God's spirit worked with people, even when unbeknownst to them, preparing sinners to receive Christ. And Wesley, too, wished to give equal time to the Christian pilgrimage toward holy living that followed justification. Somehow, the men put aside their differences and kept their friendship intact.

A Second Look at the Second Great Awakening

In the *Handbook*'s introduction, the author referred briefly to the revivalism and camp meetings that took place in America's western frontier of Kentucky and Tennessee at the beginning of the nineteenth century, drawing out certain problems. But in this chapter, he locates the revivalism in the broader context of the religious awakening that was taking place at that time, underscoring some of its positive aspects. He points to the growth of Christianity, with many declaring for the ministry; to the utopian communities that developed during that period; also, to the establishment of schools that followed; the formation of America's first missionary societies and Bible and religious literature societies; and the evangelistic activities of the circuit riders like Peter Cartwright who reached people who would not under other circumstances have been exposed to the gospel. The interest in Christian religion brought comfort to a new nation, helped unify the old colonies into a new nation, solidified the new idea of separation between state and religion, fostered ecumenical cooperation, brought a reform of morals to the frontier, took the abolitionist sentiment where it might not have under other circumstances ventured, and propelled home missions. The end of the era saw the rise of Charles Grandison Finney who, when he went to Oberlin College, directed American evangelism beyond personal conversion toward social reform, especially by providing higher education for women and Blacks.

Words of Caution

Toward the end of the chapter, the author suggests that Christians should maintain themselves vigilant about the emotionalism that often accompanies evangelism. Feeling for its own sake has little connection with Jesus' message and life. Attempting to purchase a person's commitment with false claims of blessedness and irrational hopes for wealth and good health is as equally wrongheaded as attempting to frighten a hearer into salvation. Equally pernicious, the author thinks, is the hidden imperialism, colonialism, materialism, racism, sexism, capitalism, or other -ism that sometimes accompanies evangelism. Care needs to be taken not to misuse the Bible to spread cultural values. And finally, today's evangelism should not descend into proselytizing Christians from other denominations as a way of increasing church membership. Cooperation and fellowship should mark all Christianity.

Where Do We Go from Here?

The author rejoices that Methodists and like-minded Christians enjoy a strong history of evangelism. But he also holds that important questions face twenty-first-century churches: What part of historical evangelism should we claim this century? What part should we leave behind? And what part should we modify? As a way of initiating discussion, the author holds that Christians should abhor any presentation of the faith that is disingenuous or emotionally and intellectually dishonest. Christian speech and conduct should never be deceptive or hateful. Christians should model harmony, kindness, humility, and peace. He suggests that evangelism that neglects the other's tradition is intellectually lazy and out of step with the humility demanded of anyone who speaks for God. Every use of force, coercion, compulsion, mockery, or intimidation to spread the gospel should be considered completely out of step with Christian evangelism.

Terms, Dates, Events, and People

Define, identify, or explain each word and phrase as they appear in the *Handbook*'s chapter 12. Ask your instructor or look up words or phrases that remain unclear.

- Arminianism
- Bethesda Orphan House and Academy

- Charles Grandison Finney
- connectionalism
- evangelism, evangelical, evangelicals, and evangelicalism
- George Whitefield
- gospel
- The Great Awakening
- ideology of dominion
- laity or laypersons
- Peter Cartwright
- public and social fruits of faith
- Robert Strawbridge
- Shakers
- Thomas Maxfield
- utopians
- Wesleyan spirit

Reading Comprehension

Explain these important themes found in chapter 12. Discuss them with course partners. If the *Handbook for the Christian Faith*'s author were in the room with you, what questions would you ask? Can you think of further evidence to buttress the points the author makes?

1. Evangelism simply means bringing good news to people mired in bad situations. Evangelism is what Jesus did, and it was what the apostles did.

2. John Wesley, Francis Asbury, the itinerants, the lay preachers, and early Methodist society members in general were zealous to proclaim the gospel. And early Methodism's growth in membership paralleled that of first-century Christianity.

3. The preaching of early Methodism appealed to workingmen and -women. It was religious, moral, and socially leveling.

4. The scholar Albert Outler pointed out that Methodism became a vibrant movement when Wesley became less passionate about seeking

assurance of his own salvation and more compassionate about the needs and welfare of others.

5. Wesley and early Methodism thought of the conversion experience as only the threshold of evangelism. Conversion meant changing to a new way of being and living. Early Methodism balanced the inner experience of faith with the expectation of public and social evidence for faith. The Methodist societies grew through the witness and work of laypeople.

6. George Whitefield was one of the great evangelists of the eighteenth century. Although friends with Wesley, the two disagreed strongly over slavery, over whether God's grace and the coming of Jesus was intended for only the elect or for all people, and how much importance to place on the born-again moment and the accompanying feeling of being saved.

7. The Second Great Awakening at the beginning of the nineteenth century brought rapid growth to American Christianity. It brought comfort to a new nation, helped unify the old colonies into a new nation, solidified the new idea of separation between state and religion, fostered ecumenical cooperation, brought a reform of morals to the frontier, took the abolitionist sentiment where it might not have under other circumstances ventured, and propelled home missions. It saw the development of utopian communities, the establishment of church related schools and colleges, and the formation of America's first Bible and religious literature societies.

8. As a professor and president of Oberlin College, the evangelist Charles Grandison Finney helped extend evangelism's concern beyond personal salvation to social reform. Finney's emphases included promoting higher education opportunities for women and African Americans.

9. The *Handbook*'s author suggests caution when it comes to the religious emotionalism that often accompanies evangelism, for emotionalism often disrupts rather than builds the body of Christ. Feeling for its own sake has little connection with Jesus' message and life. Attempting to purchase a person's commitment with false hopes of blessedness is as equally wrongheaded as attempting to frighten that person into salvation.

10. Evangelists face the hidden danger of allowing their own cultural values of materialism, racism, sexism, capitalism, etc. to color the gospel message. If not careful, evangelism can become an attempt at indoctrination.

11. The author raises an important task for twenty-first-century Methodists and like-minded Christians, asking, "What parts of historical evangelism should the church claim? What parts should it leave behind? And what parts should it modify?"

Exercises to Enhance Understanding

1. John Wesley organized a group of itinerant lay preachers from all walks of life who were derided by outsiders. This reflects the history of early Methodism as a lay movement led by preachers who were not ordained. Given that churches are closing, church membership is declining, and significantly fewer people are choosing to go to seminary and become ordained ministers, how might an understanding of Methodism as a lay movement inform the challenges the denomination (and all Christian churches) face today? Should any qualifications and/or educational requirements for those who become fully ordained as ministers of word and sacrament be reconsidered? If so, in what ways? Can you think of specific ways the church may have to evolve in the face of fewer ordained ministers?

2. In this chapter, the author states that "compassion is central to true evangelism." Has this been your experience of evangelical Christianity? Why or why not? How does this understanding hold up in light of the shifting understandings of what it means to be an evangelical Christian in America in this contemporary moment? In what ways do you think evangelicalism has become more aligned with political identity instead of religious faith? In pairs or as a small group, discuss specific ideas for evangelism that are creative and that may be approached with integrity today.

3. Identify and discuss any specific examples of revivalism or Great Awakenings that you see in your church or elsewhere in your community today. Are there any such movements occurring? If so, what have been their positive and negative impacts? If not, what would renewal or revivalism entail for the church today? Do you feel that such a movement is necessary in any way for the survival of the Christian church?

Suggested Readings

Boles, John B. *The Great Revival: Beginnings of the Bible Belt*. Lexington: The University Press of Kentucky, 1996.

Cushman, Robert E. "Salvation for All." In *Methodism: A Summary of Basic Information Concerning the Methodist Church*, edited William K. Anderson, 103–15. Nashville: Methodist, 1947.

Finney, Charles G. *Memoirs of Rev. Charles G. Finney Written by himself*. New York: A. B. Barnes, 1876.

Heitzenrater, Richard P. "The Revival Begins (1739–44)." In *Wesley and the People Called Methodists*, 107–52. 2nd ed. Nashville: Abingdon, 2013.

Kidd, Thomas S. *George Whitefield: America's Spiritual Founding Father*. New Haven: Yale University Press, 2016.

Outler, Albert C. *Evangelism in the Wesleyan Spirit*. Nashville: Tidings, 1971.

Sanders, Jennings B. "George Whitefield Two Hundred and Twenty-Five Years After His First American Visit: An Interpretation." *The Georgia Historical Quarterly* 48.1 (March 1964) 64–73.

Payton, Jacob S. "Methodism's Spread in America." *Methodism: A Summary of Basic Information Concerning the Methodist Church*, edited by William K. Anderson, 65–84. Nashville: Methodist, 1947.

Sherwood, Lawrence. "Growth and Spread, 1785–1804." In vol. 1 of *The History of American Methodism*, edited by Emory S. Bucke, 360–418. Nashville: Abingdon, 1964.

13

Missions

Overview and Summary of Content

THE AUTHOR BEGINS CHAPTER 13 on missions in a similar way to how he ended the previous chapter on evangelism, that is with a word of caution. Christ's work can be marred in missions when attempts to force cultural mores takes precedence over love, or when the passion for saving souls replaces a concern for the welfare and happiness of others, or when missionaries look down on traditions alien to their own experiences.

Etymology

The word "missionary" overlaps in meaning with the New Testament designation "apostle," which is rooted in the Greek verb for sending out and goes back to earliest Christianity. "Missionary" is rooted in the Latin and came into the Christian vocabulary in the sixteenth and seventeenth centuries with the Jesuit Amerindian settlements along the borderlands of Brazil, Paraguay, and Argentina. While referring to an agent or envoy sent abroad with a Christian task, the word carries the slightly broader meaning of someone who is part of an organized effort to spread religion. It also carries connotations of someone striving to enlighten a community, improve conditions of living, and Christianize society.

The Eighteenth-Century Methodist Missionary Impulse

John Wesley's and Methodism's early understanding of missions was influenced by the Church of England's missionary organization, the Society for the Propagation of the Gospel in Foreign Parts, which sent clergy to strengthen the faith of colonists and evangelize native and slave populations.

The organization provided literature, supported schools, built churches, and laid much of the foundation for what became today's Episcopal Church.

Today's Methodism does not separate preaching the gospel from responding in loving care to the personal and social needs of those hearing the gospel. But Wesley's focus was near exclusively on preaching. The church's understanding of global and home missions would develop and mature over the next two centuries. It was Thomas Coke rather than Wesley in that early period who was more enthusiastic about missions. He established Methodism first in Antigua, West Indies; was named to head the first British Methodist missionary committee; expanded the Methodist footprint into most of the islands of the West Indies, into Sierra Leone, Nova Scotia, and France; and was in the process of taking Methodism into India and South Africa when he died in 1814.

The Developing Understanding of Missions in Nineteenth-Century Protestantism

The 1800s saw growing enthusiasm for missions. The concept of missions also changed during that century. As the missionaries focused less exclusively on preaching and more on modeling a way of living, their work became also less denominational and more ecumenical, less doctrinaire and more interested in the essentials of Christianity. To illustrate, the *Handbook*'s author briefly recounts the missionary lives and exploits of David Livingstone and J. Hudson Taylor. Livingstone spent most of his life taking Christianity into Africa and Taylor into China. Besides preaching the gospel, both were medical doctors whose approach to missions was the wholistic one of improving the quality of life of the people to whom they preached. And both ended their long ministries venerated by those they felt called to serve.

Becoming One with the People

One of the ways Methodism's concept of missions developed in the nineteenth century was that it became less focused on preaching than during Wesley's day and more focused on improving the quality of life of the local people. Livingstone's impact on spreading the gospel came through his life of devotion to Africa. He lived with the people, brought modern medicine to them, and raised funds and led explorations with the goal of opening trade possibilities for the continent. Livingstone campaigned to halt African slavery. He suffered hardship, sickness, and witnessed his wife's death in Africa.

J. Hudson Taylor's influence was of a similar type. He adopted Chinese dress and ways, arguing that missionaries should affirm as much of the local culture as possible without sacrificing their Christian values. Taylor used his medical practice to heal those who were sick; he adopted an orphan as a son. He and his wife took up permanent residence in China, learned several dialects of Chinese, and translated the New Testament into the Ningbo dialect.

Nondenominational Protestant

In the missionary enterprise, there was a movement away from partisan Protestantism. The author points to the cooperation between missionaries and mission agencies. Livingstone was a Congregationalist, but he came from a Scottish Presbyterian family, was supported in his work also by evangelical Anglicans and nonconformists, and worked alongside Methodists and Baptists. J. Hudson Taylor came from a Methodist background, was most influenced as he prepared for China by the evangelical Plymouth Brethren, was first sent to China by a nondenominational Protestant society, and provided resources by Baptists and several evangelical groups. The China Inland Mission that Taylor founded embraced all leading denominations of Christians.

Meeting the Needs of People

As missionaries affirmed local culture, concentrated on the essentials of the Christian faith, and shared resources, Protestant missions (including Methodist missions) in the nineteenth century became less doctrinaire and more concerned with essentials of Christianity. The ecumenism on the mission field would expand to include Roman Catholics in the middle of the twentieth century, especially after Vatican II. By the late-twentieth century, the most vivid model of how Christian missionaries address the needs of people regardless of affiliation became Mother Teresa of Calcutta and the Missionaries of Charity who modeled the current ideal of ministering to those most in need in their place of need at their time of need.

Missions at the Core of Methodism

Certain essentials of Christian beliefs and practices are obvious on the mission field. There is the fervor for preaching the gospel, the pressing need for instruction in the faith, the reliance on prayer, the Christian witness sometimes under the stress of persecution, the close bonds among believers. Material acquisition takes second seat to compassion. Everywhere there is the exigency for education, food, clothing, medical treatment, sanitation, etc. The harsh conditions under which most people live confront the missionary with doing more than preaching a sermon and following it with an altar call.

It is in that context that the author returns to the theme of how Methodist expansion and the creation of schools were linked on the mission field. The author had described in chapter 9 that in responding to the pressing needs of Chinese and Japanese women, Mary Elizabeth Lambuth had opened schools and become something of a social reformer. She taught sanitation; insisted that those who were sick visit a doctor instead of a shaman; lobbied against certain customs that were detrimental to women, such as foot binding and concubinage; and in sum became an activist. In chapter 13, he pursues this theme further by examining the work of Annie Newman Ransom and Martha Watts in Brazil. Due largely through Methodism's work in education, within ten years the religion implanted itself in that country. By 1890, the Methodists had only constructed twenty-three church buildings but had established ten colleges and schools. By 1926, the Methodist missionaries had helped build and open forty-one schools in Brazil, sixteen being institutions of higher learning.

Christianity's Wholistic Task

The author creates the phrase "wholistic evangelism" to describe present-day missionary's work. Among Methodists and like-minded Christians, the concept of evangelism has matured from saving souls to bringing God's well-being to the whole person.

Chapter 13's last example concerns the missionary work of Al and Louise Snyder from the Free Methodist denomination in Rwanda in the 1990s. Because of a shortage, the couple came out of retirement to serve at the Kibogora hospital right as a civil war was percolating. Al kept a journal of events, making notations daily. The staff would start their day and end it with prayer and a short meditation. Among the entries are thoughts about the deeper meaning of those old Wesleyan rules to do no harm and to do good. There are references to doctors from other Christian denominations and to Roman Catholic, Presbyterian, and Baptist mission hospitals in the region. The spirit of those notations is without fail one of sharing resources, of support, of appreciation, and helping wherever there is need. There is no interest whatsoever in doctrinal differences between Christians.

As the journal progresses, the entries recount increasing violence in the Kibogora area. One month after Al and Louise arrived, there was a bombing in the town's market. He relates the chaos in the hospital as more than a hundred victims flooded in, of the triage, of the desperate attempts to save a pregnant woman and her child. Al opened one woman's chest, and blood exploded across his face. He wondered if she had AIDS. The entry for that day, May 29, 1993, was several pages long. Another entry from a few days later tells of the rape of three young teens at the Institute John Wesley, the mission school serving about thirteen hundred girls and boys. And the violence just increased from there.

The civil war escalated to the point where Al reported thousands of deaths and hundreds of thousands fleeing across the borders into refugee camps. In the course of three months, perhaps a million Tutsi and moderate Hutus were massacred. And finally, Al and Louise were forced to flee the area. Al Snyder's published journal begins with his return to Kibogora in 1995 and his sadness for friends who were no longer alive is near-overwhelming. Outler was right in his claim that compassion for a hurting world is central to evangelism. The *Handbook*'s author adds that the missionary field is everywhere the Christian's heart resides.

Where Do We Go from Here?

Methodists and like-minded Christians enjoy a strong history of missions. And the *Handbook*'s author urges twenty-first-century Methodism to keep it at the core of Christianity's tasks. Outreach is at the heart of who we are as Christians, he claims. But as with evangelism, he challenges the church to rethink its approach to missions. It cannot and should not be conducted as it was one hundred years ago when American churches raised support for missionaries who would learn a foreign language and travel to implant congregations overseas with an agenda set by US dollars and an American-staffed Board of Missions. Brotherhood, sisterhood, the sharing of talents and expertise, joint efforts, and teamwork at home and abroad mark the path for future missions. And the author reminds us that the world has shrunk to the extent that we are not only brothers and sisters in Christ. We are next-door neighbors. He urges Christians to reconceive missions for this century by dropping every pretense of superiority over God's children from other corners of the world.

Terms, Dates, Events, and People

Define, identify, or explain each word and phrase as they appear in the *Handbook*'s chapter 13. Ask your instructor or look up words or phrases that remain unclear.

- missions and missionaries
- apostle
- catechize
- David Livingstone
- James Hudson Taylor
- Jesuits or Society of Jesus
- Reverend Junius Newman
- Society for the Propagation of the Gospel in Foreign Parts
- Vatican II
- Vulgate Bible
- wholistic evangelism

Reading Comprehension

Explain these important themes found in chapter 13. Discuss them with course partners. If the *Handbook for the Christian Faith*'s author were in the room with you, what questions would you ask? Can you think of further evidence to buttress the points the author makes?

1. Christ's work can be marred when missionaries attempt to force their cultural values on those they are called to serve. Love and compassion are at the heart of successful missions. Concern for the welfare and happiness of others should guide the missionary's passion for saving souls. Missionaries should be careful not to look down glibly on traditions alien to their own.

2. The term missionary has a broader meaning than the term evangelist. It denotes one who is part of an organized effort to spread religion. It

also carries connotations of someone striving to enlighten a community, improve living conditions, and Christianize society.

3. John Wesley's view of missionary work was influenced by both the New Testament stories of Paul's preaching in Acts and by the Church of England's missionary organization, the Society for the Propagation of the Gospel in Foreign Parts. Wesley focused largely on preaching, which he mainly directed at English-speaking colonists.

4. Thomas Coke was the early Methodist who was most enthusiastic about missions. Coke established Methodism first in Antigua and later in most of the islands of the West Indies. He headed British Methodism's first missionary committee; took Methodism to Sierra Leone, Nova Scotia, and France; and was in the process of taking it to India and South Africa when he died. John Stewart, who took Christianity to the Delaware and Wyandot Native Americans, was American Methodism's first missionary.

5. The Protestant concept of missions matured during the nineteenth century when missionary activity became less focused exclusively on preaching and more directed toward modeling a way of living. It also became less denominational and more ecumenical; less doctrinaire and more interested in the essentials of Christianity.

6. The *Handbook*'s author uses David Livingstone and J. Hudson Taylor to illustrate the changes that occurred in Protestant missions during the nineteenth century. Livingstone spent most of his life in Africa; Taylor, in China. Besides being preachers, both were medical doctors devoted to improving living conditions for the people they were called to serve.

7. J. Hudson Taylor adopted Chinese clothes, shaved his forehead, and braided his hair into a queue. He taught that missionaries should adopt as much local culture as possible without sacrificing their Christian values.

8. An ecumenical *rapprochement* between Roman Catholics and Protestants occurred during the middle of the twentieth century with Pope John XXIII and Vatican II. By the end of the twentieth century, Mother Teresa of Calcutta and the Missionaries of Charity had become models for how Christians should address the needs of people regardless of religious affiliation. Missionaries minister to those most in need in their place of need at their time of need.

9. The wholistic task of Christian ministry is obvious on the mission field. There we find fervor for preaching the gospel, a pressing need for instruction in the faith, reliance on prayer, Christian witness sometimes under stress of persecution, and close bonds among believers all in measure not ordinarily seen. Likewise, the social needs of the poor are more visible. Material acquisition takes second seat to compassion. Everywhere there is the exigency for education, food, clothing, medical treatment, sanitation, etc.

10. Education and creating schools have been an important part of Methodist missions. In the last half of the nineteenth and first half of the twentieth centuries, missionary women, in particular, played a role as social reformers by responding to the needs of the women they encountered in conservative Asian and Latin American societies.

11. Preaching and the implantation of churches have from earliest times been important missionary tasks. But the concept of evangelism in the mission field broadened to include bringing God's well-being to the whole person. For Methodists and like-minded Christians, today's missionary activity is a wholistic task.

12. The *Handbook*'s author holds that outreach, sharing the good news with the nations, teaching what the Lord commanded, loving God, loving the neighbor, and doing good are in the DNA of Methodism. But he also suggests that missionary activity today must be different from what it was one hundred years ago. The idea of US dollars and an American-staffed Board of Missions setting the contours and agenda for ministry in other countries is out-of-step with our times. Teamwork at home and abroad mark the path for future missions.

Exercises to Enhance Understanding

1. What tends to be the missionary focus in your own church or congregation? Does your own church mostly support mission work that occurs in other parts of the world or does it mostly attend to local needs in your own community? Should churches have a balance in terms of the types of mission efforts that they support? In pairs or in a small group, discuss specific examples of missions that are supported by your congregation.

2. Given our contemporary understanding of the negative impacts of colonialism, in what ways does our understanding of missions need

to change, if at all? Discuss what missionary work ought to look like in our contemporary world. What should be the role of Christian missionaries who feel called to travel to other countries to do such work?

3. In pairs or in a small group, share any stories and experiences you have had with missions. Have you participated in missionary work in another community or in another country? What was rewarding about that experience? What was problematic? In what ways did the experience reflect the gospel?

Suggested Readings

From the Bible: The book of Acts 13–23.

Coke, Thomas. "Address to the Pious and Benevolent, Proposing an Annual Subscription for the Support of Missionaries in the Highlands and Adjacent Islands of Scotland, the Isles of Jersey, Guernsey, and Newfoundland, the West Indies, and the Provinces of Nova Scotia and Quebec." London, 1786. https://open.bu.edu/bitstream/handle/2144/662/Thomas%20Coke%20-%20An%20Address%20to%20the%20Pious%20and%20Benevolent.pdf?sequence=2.

Hogg, W. Richey. "The Missions of American Methodism." In vol. 3 of *The History of American Methodism*, Edited by Emory S. Bucke, 59–128. Nashville: Abingdon, 1964.

Jeal, Tim. *Livingstone: Revised and Expanded Edition*. New Haven: Yale University Press, 2013.

Maughan, W. Somerset. "Rain." In *Rain and Other Stories*, by W. Somerset Maughan, 115–47. New York: Grosset & Dunlap, 1921.

Scott, David, and Thomas Kemper, eds. *Methodist Missions at 200: Serving Faithfully Amid the Tensions*. Nashville: Abingdon, 2021.

Taylor, James Hudson. *To China with Love: The Only Autobiographical Writing of J. Hudson Taylor*. 17th ed. Minneapolis: Bethany Fellowship, 1972. Originally issued under the title *A Retrospect* (London: China Inland Mission, 1894).

14

Church and World

Doing Good

Overview and Summary of Content

IN AUGUST 1730, JOHN Wesley and other members of the Holy Club began visitations to debtors and felons at Castle Prison in Oxford. And soon they also set up a program extending help to poor children and others in the city. Wesley affirmed that works of mercy are necessary and if neglected Christians would not receive all the grace that God intends for people. And he also suggested that one of the reasons wealthy people are often insensitive to the poor is that they seldom visit them. People of means, he thought, should address the physical needs of the poor even before they address spiritual needs. And if not wealthy, Christians should visit anyway, addressing spiritual needs.

Acts of Mercy and the First Benevolences

Requirements for those participating in the earliest Methodist societies included financial contributions, a portion of which was allocated for the poor. Emphasis was given to teaching poor children, assisting the sick, and visiting prisoners. At first, these were acts of individual conscience. Wesley himself had the custom of fasting, often twice each week, and donating money otherwise used for his meals for the poor. But in Wesley's Foundery, providing food, clothing, shelter, and medical care soon became institutionalized, spreading to all Methodist societies and classes.

Mercy to Prisoners

Wesley considered prisons the places closest to hell one could find on earth. The poor were often imprisoned for as little as two weeks' wages. The justice system of the day did not think in terms of rehabilitating criminals. Prisoners were kept in squalid conditions until their debts were paid. If holding a job, debtors were allowed to leave for work during daylight hours and from their wages, they paid rent to the prison and purchased food. A portion of their earnings was subtracted each week to pay down their outside debt. If not able to afford the rent and dependent on family and friends to pay their debt, the paupers were crowded twenty-four seven into a common area and fed by charity when food was available. Starvation and sickness were common. Wesley not only preached to those incarcerated but campaigned for better conditions for the prisoners. He was especially concerned about women with small children being held crowded together with criminals of all kinds. Wesley so constantly criticized conditions that he was banned from appearing for periods of time at certain prisons.

Mercy to Children

Sunday school developed with the purposes of training working-class children in Christian morality and teaching them to read, write, and cipher numbers. Since Sunday was the children-chimney sweeps', hawkers of wares', carriage runners', house maids', and factory workers' only time off during the week, that became the time of schooling. Beyond instruction, Sunday school provided the added benefit of taking the children away from mischief on city streets.

The Anglican newspaper proprietor from Gloucester, Robert Raikes, is the person most associated today with the Sunday school movement, but the schools seemed to have been first initiated by Methodists and were mostly found among them. In Gloucester, a young Methodist woman named Sarah Cook began teaching the children who worked in her father's pin factory to read and write before marching them down to a Christian worship service held on Sundays by the headmaster of the Cathedral School. It was probably through Sarah Cook that Raikes first became involved in Sunday school. Sunday schooling provided possibilities for advancement unknown before among working-class people. While the Church of England, the government, and several leading figures at first hesitated, they soon supported Raikes's work. A Sunday school society was formed in 1805 to promote the movement. By 1818, five hundred thousand poor children were being helped through Sunday schools. By the end of the nineteenth century, that number had increased to over seven and a half million.

Church Benevolences

Christian denominations create structures for doing good. Methodists and like-minded Protestant churches raise money to carry out programs of ministry, evangelism, missions, and acts of mercy. In the United Methodist Church these are called benevolences and many churches have established local programs that provide assistance for those in need—food, clothing, and emergency relief; help for the homeless; and help for those struggling with addiction, victims of spousal abuse, or simply people in need of counseling. Christians should be encouraged by the good that can be accomplished simply by organizing to do good. The ability to structure doing good is one of the advantages that denominations have over single congregations.

Church-Related Institutions

In this chapter, the author picks up again on the theme of how Methodism's influence was strongly felt through the development of church-related schools, making the further point that typically church-related schools and similar institutions have originated from community leaders joining forces with the church to meet community needs. Some of the most prestigious universities in our own country arose in this manner. Methodists and like-minded Christians have attempted to take seriously Jesus' direction to love God with all of one's mind; they have wanted to be useful to God and God's purposes and the opportunities to be of benefit to God increase with schooling; and institutions of learning have arisen from the desire to do good—that is from the desire to help their local community, providing expertise, opportunities for betterment, economic development, and a multitude of other benefits that accompany a better educated citizenry.

Besides colleges and universities, there are several renowned medical and nursing schools and hospitals historically related to American Methodism. American Methodists have also established or helped establish numerous orphanages and homes for elder care. The missions of these institutions meet Wesleyan standards of service, generosity, mercy, and kindness.

Christian-Inspired Nonprofit Organizations

Besides institutions of mercy that are institutionally and/or historically related to the church, many Methodists and like-minded Christians participate in allied charitable organizations. These are too numerous to list, but the author provides a sampling—the YMCA, the Red Cross, the Salvation Army, Habitat for Humanity—pausing long enough on each to show their Christian activist origins. Although these organizations are fully part of secular society now, the Christian impulse to do good remains very much visible.

The Social Gospel

As individuals and as societies of believers, eighteenth- and nineteenth-century Methodists and like-minded Christians were agents of change. They rallied their members for social betterment; they organized community efforts; and they raised money and organized support to build schools, hospitals, soup kitchens, orphanages, and elder care facilities. And that generosity extended overseas.

In the late-nineteenth and early-twentieth centuries, a young Baptist professor at Rochester Theological Seminary, Walter Rauschenbusch, argued that many of the problems his parishioners faced resulted from the way society was organized. The monopolization of land and other natural resources by some, for instance, while perfectly legal, was nevertheless unjust because it violated God's desire that creation benefit all. Sin was more than an individual transgression. Sin was also transmitted through culture, customs, traditions, and unjust laws. Collective sin was present in super-personal forces like war and the industrial greed of capitalism. The social gospel called for more direct activism on the part of Christians and the church to restructure society away from power, violence, and greed to Christian ideals.

The Methodist Harry F. Ward tended to think of a laundry list of issues that brought about social injustice. The "Social Creed of Methodism" was penned and adopted in 1908, and that creed in turn became the model for the many Protestant denominations. The Social Principles of the United Methodist Church and similar Protestant denominations today were born out of this movement.

Liberation Theology

Like the social gospel, liberation theology developed from the realization that sin works not just through individuals but also through macro societal structures. Christians marching to bring political, cultural, and economic change to the unjust segregated society of mid-twentieth century America was exactly what occurred with the Southern Christian Leadership Conference's role in the civil rights movement of the 1960s. In 1970, the Methodist (AME Church) theologian James H. Cone argued that Black theology should reject the White supremacy that colored so much Western theology and emphasize instead Jesus' message of liberation to oppressed people.

Near the same time, the Roman Catholic council of Latin American bishops was urging the church to take a more active role publicly in overcoming the widespread torture, violence, and poverty in their countries. They saw an institutional Christianity that was standing by mute as human rights were abused. They called for the church to become active in liberating people from the economic and sociopolitical conditions that oppressed them. These conditions included the actions of nation states and multinational corporations. The poverty of poorer nations often directly resulted from economic and political structures that favored the rich and powerful. Sometimes the poverty, violence, and oppression that followed were rooted inside those nations but often also outside the borders of those nations.

Where Do We Go from Here?

Methodists and like-minded Christians are tasked with being instruments for good. The efforts of individuals are multiplied exponentially in groups. How to go about doing good? In a play on words, the author suggests that we become the company we keep. And beginning with Jesus, the pioneer and perfecter of our faith, the history of Christianity has surrounded us with a great cloud of witnesses. Members of our church family and people of goodwill throughout the world provide models for doing good. And you and I are asked to model good for those who follow. One way to think of Christianity is that it liberates people to do good. Christians can work with the talents that God bestowed on each person to do good. And all of us were given the most important talent, that of sharing love.

Terms, Dates, Events, and People

Define, identify, or explain each word and phrase as they appear in the *Handbook*'s chapter 14. Ask your instructor or look up words or phrases that remain unclear.

- apportionments
- benevolences
- colonialism
- Dwight L. Moody
- Sir George Williams
- Henry Dunant
- the Industrial Revolution
- liberation theology
- Marshalsea Prison and Newgate Prison
- *Pacem in Terris*
- *Populorum Progressio*
- The Red Cross
- *Rerum Novarum*
- Robert Raikes
- the Salvation Army
- social gospel
- Sunday school movement
- United Methodist Social Principles
- William Booth and Catherine Mumford
- works of mercy as means of grace
- Young Men's Christian Association

Reading Comprehension

Explain these important themes found in chapter 14. Discuss them with course partners. If the *Handbook for the Christian Faith*'s author were in the room with you, what questions would you ask? Can you think of further evidence to buttress the points the author makes?

1. John Wesley thought that works of mercy were a means of grace. If not performed, Christians would not receive all the grace that God intends for people. When works of mercy were neglected, Christians became weaker in faith.

2. Requirements for participating in the earliest Methodist societies included financial contributions. A portion of the monies raised was allocated for the poor, hungry, thirsty, stranger, naked, sick, and those in prison. Each society appointed lay stewards who oversaw the collection and its use. Emphasis was given to teaching poor children, assisting the sick, and visiting prisoners.

3. Wesley not only preached to those incarcerated but campaigned for better conditions for prisoners. With regard to debtors, he was especially concerned about women with small children held crowded together with criminals of all kinds. Wesley so criticized prison conditions that he was banned from appearing for periods of time at certain prisons.

4. Sunday school developed with the purposes of training working-class children in Christian morality and teaching them to read, write, and cipher numbers. Since Sunday was the only time off for children—chimney sweeps, hawkers of wares, carriage runners, house maids, and factory workers, that became the time of schooling. A Sunday school society was formed in 1805 to promote the movement. By 1818, half a million poor children were being helped through Sunday schools. By the end of the nineteenth century, that number had increased to 7.5 million.

5. Christian denominations create structures for doing good. Methodists and like-minded Protestant churches raise money to carry out works of mercy. Many churches provide assistance for those in need—food, clothing, and emergency relief. Christians and non-Christians can find help if they are homeless, struggling with addictions, victims of spousal or partner abuse, or simply in need of counseling.

6. Church-related schools and other institutions often originated from community leaders joining forces with churches to meet community needs. Schools have provided expertise, opportunities for betterment, economic development, a better educated citizenry, and other benefits to their communities.

7. The Christian impulse to do good stands behind the establishment of some famous nonprofit organizations. These include the YMCA, the Red Cross, the Salvation Army, and Habitat for Humanity.

8. Rauschenbusch and the social gospel recognized the social dimension of sin. The very way that society is organized can produce social ills. Sin can be transmitted through culture, customs, traditions, and unjust laws. The social gospel calls for Christian activism to change unjust laws, social mores, and community practices.

9. The 1963 encyclical *Pacem in Terris* claimed that real peace on earth would come when people and governments fully respected the human rights that God intended for all people. These included the rights to bodily integrity and to the means necessary to preserve and develop life; to food, clothing, medical care, shelter, necessary social services, disability aid; to respect and to their own liberty, to education and to worship, to choose freely a state of life and to have support in bringing up a family; to work, to the ownership of property, to free association, to travel, and to take part in public life. The document further affirmed that every right carried a corresponding duty.

10. Liberation theology holds that economic and sociopolitical structures can be demonic in the sense that they can lead to torture, repression, violence, and poverty. In solidarity with oppressed people, the church should become an instrument of liberation and justice.

11. God expects Christians to do good everywhere within their reach. Christianity frees people to do good. People have been given talents explicitly to help them be useful to God by doing good. While some people have been gifted with many talents, every person has been gifted with the greatest single talent, the ability to share love.

Exercises to Enhance Understanding

1. One of John Wesley's "works of mercy" involved visiting the incarcerated and working for better prison conditions. Although jail and prison ministry opportunities exist, there has been an increase in residential programs that provide support and assistance to help reduce recidivism, specifically among those suffering from addiction. Spend time seeking out and identifying any prison ministries or similar residential programs in your own community. What information can you find? What can you learn about them? How do such programs benefit your community or region? Are you or is your church involved in either a prison ministry or a ministry that supports men and women once they are released?

2. Think about your experiences, especially as a child, in Sunday school. What role did weekly lessons play in your faith formation? What are some of your memories of these experiences? Many smaller, mainline Protestant churches no longer offer Sunday school or other organized learning opportunities for children, teens, or adults. In pairs or in a small group, discuss the implications and impacts of this shift in religious education.

3. It is clear that many people find in the gospel a call to work actively toward addressing issues of economic and social justice. From your perspective, in what ways is such work the responsibility of the Christian church, if at all? In pairs or as a small group, discuss the ways a clearer focus on these matters might reshape the identity of the church. Do you think this could provide impetus for a renewed and reinvigorated Christianity? What would this look like for local congregations like your own?

Suggested Readings

Brown, Robert McAfee. *Liberation Theology: An Introductory Guide*. Louisville: Westminster/John Knox, 1993.

Carter, Henry. "The Social Obligations of the Inheritance." In *The Methodist Heritage*, 111–29. Nashville: Abingdon-Cokesbury, 1951.

Evans, Christopher H. *The Social Gospel in American Religion: A History*. New York: New York University Press, 2017.

Hanks, Geoffrey. *60 Great Founders*. Bristol: Christian Focus, 1995.

Hosier, Helen K. *William and Catherine Booth: Founders of the Salvation Army*. Heroes of the Faith. Uhrichsville, OH: Barbour, 1999.

John XXIII, Pope. "*Pacem in Terris* (1963)." In *Proclaiming Justice and Peace: Papal Documents from Rerum Novarum through Centesimus Annus*, edited by Michael Walsh and Brian Davies, 125–56. Rev. and exp. ed. Mystic, CT: Twenty-Third, 1991.

Muelder, Walter G. "Methodism's Contribution to Social Reform." In *Methodism: A Summary of Basic Information Concerning the Methodist Church*, edited William K. Anderson, 192–205. Nashville: Methodist, 1947.

Murdock, Norman H. *Origins of the Salvation Army*. Eugene: OR: Wipf and Stock, 2014.

Rauschenbusch, Walter. *A Theology for the Social Gospel (1917)*. Whitefish, MT: Kessinger, 2008.

The United Methodist Church (UMC). *The Social Principles*. General Board of Church and Society for The United Methodist Church. Nashville: United Methodist, 1996.

15

The Church as Church

The Nature and Institutional Structure of the Church, Church Governance, and Organization

Overview and Summary of Content

THE *HANDBOOK*'S CHAPTER 15 opens with the question, what makes the church church? Most Christian affirmations of faith include brief statements about the church. For example, the Nicene Creed contains the description of the church as holy, catholic, and apostolic. And to that, historical Methodism at its founding at the 1784 Christmas Conference added that the visible church is a congregation of faithful men in which the pure word of God is preached and the sacraments administered.

The Apostolic Churches

There is a historical problem in describing the church in that it lies between two determinative events, the historical appearance of Christ in the first century and the expected judgment at the end of time. While the old age with corruption, injustice, sickness, and death are still very much present in the church as in the world, the church at the same time is holy. The church anticipates the coming age, and within the church reigns the pure love of God. Also, a problem when describing the church is that early Christianity showed little interest in describing its nature and organization. Our understanding of what the New Testament writers thought needs to be culled from their comments about other topics.

Church Models

Other than accidental information about the church from Paul's letters and other early Christian writings, we have at our disposal models of how groups of people were organized in the first century Mediterranean world. The author mentions four models: the *household* was broader than our extended family in modern Western society and would have included slaves, freed servants, hired workers, and sometimes tenants and business associates; *voluntary associations*, especially burial societies; *diaspora synagogues*; and *the philosophical schools*, namely stoicism. All of these organizations shared group dynamics akin to family connections, providing a strong inside-outside dimension to local churches. When joining the church, old ties were broken; Christians became part of a new family.

Church Leadership in the Apostolic Age

Church governance in early Christianity is likewise sketchy. The New Testament writings mention the commissioning of the twelve disciples to be judges over the twelve tribes, the apostles, the council in Jerusalem, ministerial teams, and leadership in local churches. In the late New Testament period, the positions of bishops, elders, and deacons grew in importance. And the author indicates that the ordering of these titles into holy orders became clearer in the second-century church, especially with Ignatius of Antioch. That hierarchy consisted of first, bishops; second, elders (or priests); and third, deacons.

Where first-century Christian writings focused directly on the nature and organization of the church, aspects that received most attention were the boundaries of practice and belief. There were concerns about divisions in the church. The attempt was to be inclusive and maintain unity in the midst of diversity but, when necessary, Paul and other early Christian leaders instructed that certain practices and beliefs were out-of-bounds. In the second century, the concept of apostolic succession became increasingly important, until finally tying authentic Christianity in the West to a deposit of faith located especially in churches founded by the apostles.

The Hierarchical Church of the Middle Ages

As Christianity moved from being a persecuted minority to becoming the dominant religion in Europe beginning in the fourth century, emphasis shifted toward clear statements of beliefs and practices. The affirmation of a united, universal church whose main beliefs descended from the apostles became authoritative for Christianity of the Middle Ages. Membership in the church occurred with baptism. A hierarchical ordering for the church solidified. The status of males increased while that of females decreased. Dissenting groups were moved to the periphery.

The model of church that dominated the early Middle Ages was that of the Ark of Salvation. The world was dangerous and transitory, and Christians saw themselves on a journey to their true home in heaven. The church was a place of safety and a conduit to salvation. The church's participation in society was oriented in large measure to maintaining its role as a vessel to the next life. During the High Middle Ages and Late Middle Ages, the symbol of the Ark gave way to that of the cathedral. Cathedrals, when seen from the city street, recall fortresses. From inside the building, believers glimpsed heaven. But observed from a hill overlooking a medieval town, the cathedral also symbolizes power and prominence.

The Sixteenth Century and the Reformed Church

The church's approximation to secular government and its investment in power and wealth led to extensive corruption. And in large measure, it was the church's venality that most drove the Protestant Reformation. After recounting main elements of Martin Luther's confrontation with the church in Rome, the *Handbook*'s author points out that the upheaval of northern Europe led to rethinking the nature and organization of the church. The Reformation and the ensuing wars shook the accepted view in the West of the church's universal unity and of a true apostolic succession in spiritual matters. What emerges in the Lutheran statements about the church that followed are emphases on community, the preaching of the gospel, and a desire to recapture the purity of early Christianity. The Lutherans also adopted Augustine of Hippo's view of an invisible but true church inside of the visible church.

In Geneva, John Calvin pushed the Protestant concept of the community of the saints further than had Luther and his followers, emphasizing that the church is composed of the elect people of God. While not free from sin, the elect are of one body, the body of Christ, and of one spirit. The church is a covenant community, its members joined in purpose with Christ. Calvin also went further than Luther in thinking that the Scriptures provided clear directions for the organization of the visible church, the extension of its rule into society, and for norms of Christian conduct.

To the south, in what today is Spain, Isabella of Castile was also interested in church purity. But instead of breaking with Rome, she and Ferdinand sought to purify both the church and their subjects. They used the Inquisition to root out doctrinal heresy. And equally important they sought the church's help in instructing and nurturing the right customs and morals. At first, this concept of the church as mother and teacher applied mainly to Isabella's and the church's subjects in Spain and the New World. But the concept soon became descriptive also for the church's relationship to the elite of society. While not having the power to impose authority on sovereigns, the church used its persuasive powers. Schooling children who someday would be rulers became an important function of the church.

The Middle Path of the Church of Elizabethan England

Elizabeth I came to rule at a time when the English people were divided over religion. Many of the kingdom's noblemen, bishops, and its monastic communities leaned toward keeping strong ties with the church of Rome. Meanwhile, the merchants and businessmen in London and the seaports had Protestant leanings. Elizabeth chose a path whereby in outward appearance the church remained in large measure Roman Catholic but in its theology was more Protestant than Catholic. Elizabeth herself remained as head of the Church of England. And as long as her rule was not contested, the government accepted limited religious toleration.

Wesleyan Methodism's Church

John Wesley and American Methodism adopted from the Church of England the view that the church is a congregation of faithful men in which the word of God is preached and the sacraments administered. Worship was simple. Methodist meetings were marked by heartfelt prayers, the singing of hymns, lay Bible readings, some female leadership, discussions about community and individual needs, open confessions of sins, exhortations to do good, and personal testimonies. We see a return to the group dynamics of the first Christians. The founding presence of Wesley and then Asbury in America; the itinerancy of the preachers; the lay involvement in local leadership; and the bonding that occurred in the meetings where members' personal investment in each other's lives could be descriptive of the Apostle Paul's first-century churches.

Besides the simplicity of worship, early Methodism separated from the Church of England in the way it was organized. Tensions arose with

Wesley's recruitment of lay preachers, who were not certified by the Church of England. In early days, Wesley maintained that the sacraments should be administered only by the ordained clergy of the Church of England. But that necessarily changed after the War of Independence when American Methodism could no longer respond to a church headed by the King of England. The institutional break between Methodists and the Church of England in Britain would occur only after Wesley's death. The founding Christmas Conference in 1784 also saw American Methodism add a spirit of democracy and the involvement and authority of the Conference to church governance.

Where Do We Go from Here?

In a section toward the end of the chapter the *Handbook*'s author provides summary statements concerning the nature of the church, the marks of the church, the composition of the church, and the task of the church. He reminds us that the church stands between the times but is rooted in the event of Jesus and anticipates the coming kingdom of God. He urges twenty-first-century Christians to recapture important facets of the church's self-understanding.

Small, tightly knit groups characterized both the first Christian churches and early Methodism. Adherents considered themselves to be a new family in Christ. During its early centuries, Christianity stressed the unity of the church—being one body of Christ. Leaders affirmed the apostolic roots of the church and were more interested in inclusion than exclusion.

The Lutheran Reformation saw northern European Christians back away from the corruption of money and power that had gained a foothold in the church. Luther and the Protestants emphasized the word of God, the sacraments, and being a faithful community. In Calvin's Geneva and again with the Wesleyan movement, much attention was given to holiness.

Queen Isabella's Spain came to see Christianity as intolerant of heresy but also as a mother and teacher. And a constant theme in the *Handbook* is that contemporary Christianity needs to do better work instructing the faith. With Elizabeth's Church of England, there was a move toward being a more tolerant church. The author urges that an ecumenical approach characterize Christianity in the twenty-first century. And finally, he points out that all the definitions for church that emerged in the overview held to an orderly church.

Terms, Dates, Events, and People

Define, identify, or explain each word and phrase as they appear in the *Handbook*'s chapter 15. Ask your instructor or look up words or phrases that remain unclear.

- already, but not yet
- apostolic deposit of faith
- Ark of Salvation
- Augsburg Confession
- *Book of Common Prayer*
- burial societies
- catholic and apostolic church and Roman Catholic Church
- commissioning
- Constantine the Great
- Council of Nicaea
- covenant community
- deacons, elders, and bishops
- Hellenists
- holy kiss
- indulgences
- Medici family
- model of household
- Nicene Creed
- the Ninety-Five Theses
- papal states
- philosophical schools
- Spanish Inquisition
- transubstantiation
- voluntary associations

Reading Comprehension

Explain these important themes found in chapter 15. Discuss them with course partners. If the *Handbook for the Christian Faith*'s author were in the room with you, what questions would you ask? Can you think of further evidence to buttress the points the author makes?

1. Since the first Christians expected Christ's imminent return and reign, the New Testament writers did not leave a guidebook describing the nature and organization of the church. Nevertheless, certain aspects about what makes the church church can be culled from the writers' comments about other topics.

2. Wayne Meeks's *The First Urban Christians* describes first century models for early churches. He mentions the household; voluntary associations, such as burial societies; diaspora synagogues; and philosophical schools, namely Stoicism. What these models shared with the emerging church were group dynamics akin to family connections.

3. Early church leadership included apostles, a council in Jerusalem, and ministerial teams. During the late New Testament period, the positions of bishops, elders, and deacons grew in importance.

4. Early Christian writers were concerned about divisions in the church. The Apostle Paul argued for unity and preferred inclusion to exclusion. His letters show that it was when disagreements compelled responses, he and other Christian leaders stepped in and instructed that certain views and behaviors were out of bounds.

5. During the Middle Ages, European Christianity adopted an institutional structure patterned on and buttressed by imperial rule. Prominent religious leaders working in concert with secular rulers affirmed a united, universal church whose main beliefs descended from the apostles.

6. The church's approximation to secular government and its investment in power and wealth led to extensive corruption in Christianity. The Reformer Martin Luther helped lead a protest movement that emphasized community, preaching the gospel, and a return to church purity. Luther thought that while there are hypocrites and evil people who mingle in the visible church, the real church is properly a congregation of saints and true believers.

7. The Reformer John Calvin wished for less room for hypocrites and false believers in the visible church. He held that the visible church should be a body of the elect of God and that reception of God's word should mark the lives of believers. The Scriptures provided directions

for the organization of the visible church, for the extension of the church's rule into society, and for norms of Christian conduct.

8. Isabella of Castile emphasized the church's functions of teaching and nurturing morals and customs. At first, this concept of the church as a mother and teacher was applied to Isabella's simple subjects. But especially in the New World, the church soon extended its influence into society through schools for the elite, training children who would someday become rulers.

9. Under Elizabeth I the Church of England mixed aspects of Roman Catholic liturgy and worship with a theology that was more Protestant than Roman Catholic. This middle path represented a small step toward religious toleration—so long as the authority of the Queen as head of the church was not questioned.

10. Besides preaching, early Methodist meetings were marked by heartfelt prayers, the singing of hymns, lay Bible readings, some female leadership, discussions about community and individual needs, open confession of sins, exhortations to do good, and personal testimonies. Worship was simpler than in the Church of England. Outward appearances gave way to inner holiness and practicality.

11. American Methodism officially separated from the Church of England, following political independence from the crown and king's church. That took place at the Christmas Conference of 1784. The new church added a spirit of democracy and the involvement and authority of the conference to church governance. As American Methodism developed and expanded, it continued to combine hierarchical with democratic-representative aspects of governance.

Exercises to Enhance Understanding

1. "The church is not a building, the church is not a steeple, the church is not a resting place, the church is a people" reads a verse from "We Are the Church," a hymn found in the *United Methodist Hymnal*. Consider together whether this verse accurately reflects perceptions held by most people of what the church is and does. What are some things you have heard or overheard from neighbors and acquaintances about Christianity and the Christian church, in general? Are perceptions of Christianity in your community largely positive or negative? Can you think of or identify other hymns that provide an understanding of what the church should be?

2. The COVID-19 pandemic altered many things about the church as we know it. Churches that did not previously offer online or live-streamed experiences quickly made changes so that congregants could participate in worship online instead of in-person, and such virtual options are now an expectation. What other changes are occurring in worship because of this new reality in church attendance? What have been the positive and negative implications of this shift for your own congregation? In pairs or in small groups, list and discuss specific ideas for ways church members can connect with each other and build and maintain relationships both in-person and in virtual spaces? What possibilities for the church does this new reality offer?

3. If your own church ceased to exist, how would that affect you and your faith? How would it impact the community in which you live, if at all? Is attending church and participating in corporate worship a primary and necessary element of your own faith? Would you seek out another place of worship to attend? In pairs or as a group, imagine that you have an opportunity to create an ideal church. What would this church be like? What would worship look like? What role would the church play in the community through specific programs, missions, or outreach?

Suggested Readings

Bettensen, Henry, and Chris Maunder, eds. *Documents of the Christian Church*. 3rd ed. Oxford: Oxford University Press, 1999.

Boff, Leonardo. *Church, Charism, and Power. Liberation Theology and the Institutional Church*. Translated by John W. Diercksmeier. New York: Crossroad, 1985.

DeWolf, C. Harold. "The Doctrine of the Church." In *Methodism: A Summary of Basic Information Concerning the Methodist Church*, edited by William K. Anderson, 217–28. Nashville: Methodist, 1947.

Heitzenrater, Richard P. "Tensions and Transitions (1775–92)." *Wesley and the People Called Methodists*, 313–34. 2nd ed. Nashville: Abingdon, 2013.

Hillerbrand, Hans J., ed. *The Protestant Reformation*. New York: Harper and Row, 1968.

Kärkkäinen, Veli-Matti. *An Introduction to Ecclesiology: Ecumenical Historical and Global Perspectives*. Downers Grove, IL: IVP Academic, 2002.

Meeks, Wayne A. *The First Urban Christians: The Social World of the Apostle Paul*. New Haven: Yale University Press, 2003.

Outler, Albert C., ed. "Church and Sacraments." In *John Wesley*, 306–44. New York: Oxford University Press, 1980.

Williams, Colin W. "The Doctrine of the Church." In *John Wesley's Theology Today: A Study of the Wesleyan Tradition in the Light of Current Theological Dialogue*, 141–66. Nashville: Abingdon, 1960.

Conclusion

An Agenda for Contemporary Methodists and Like-Minded Protestants

Overview and Summary of Content

IN THE *HANDBOOK*'S CONCLUDING pages, the author returns to some questions raised at the beginning of the book. Is religion vanishing from American life? As he explains, the concern goes far beyond the shrinking membership among Methodists and similar Christian denominations. For, the disappearance of essential Christian values in American society is already affecting Americans' sense of purpose, fulfillment, and happiness. The loss, he thinks, is reducing the possibility of greater brotherhood and sisterhood in church and society in our nation. And so he asks, can the trend be reversed? Can American Methodists and like-minded Christians rediscover their spiritual identity? And if so, how?

The busy lives that most people lead along with the materialism of the present age have pushed spiritual concerns into the background. Volunteerism and other characteristics of American Christianity have allowed the unwitting introduction of poorly considered cultural values into religion. Emphases on the conversion experience and the feeling of salvation that accompany much of American Christianity have in unintended ways undermined community.

The most common patterns of Sunday worship today among Methodists and like-minded Protestants are directed at creating emotional responses among worshipers. Too often missing in worship is instruction in the faith. The virtual disappearance of adult Sunday school classes, mid-week prayer meetings, and clergy-led reading and discussion groups has exacerbated the problem. Anecdotal stories from ministers, nationwide surveys of religious knowledge, denominational membership records, and statistical evidence from church attendance polls show that American Christianity is failing the task of nurturing growth in the Christian faith.

An Agenda

Reading the *Handbook for the Christian Faith* can be a journey of discovery. What are the essential beliefs and practices of Christianity? These aren't two different things. For beliefs and practices walk hand in hand. "No good tree bears bad fruit, nor again does a bad tree bear good fruit; for each tree is known by its own fruit" (Luke 6:43–44). Or to quote Jesus again, "For where your treasure is, there your heart will be also" (Matt 6:21).

Beyond more knowledge about Christianity, the author wishes to help fellow travelers recommit to a Christian philosophy of living. But how to get beyond understanding Christianity as a religion to an essential understanding of ourselves as Christians? What ultimately leads to spiritual and church renewal?

Here are the concrete steps the author suggests that Methodists and like-minded Protestants take:

Suggestion #1. Let's Take Time to Be Holy

The author suggests that Christians attend to their spiritual health by, first, spending more time with God. Christianity affirms that people have become alienated from their true selves, the world God created, and the divine. But that separation need not be final. God has already acted. People's response includes repentance, which entails contrition, confession, and taking steps toward a new life. And the part we most often ignore is the last part, the doing of the new life. The author suggests building habits of personal holiness, which include prayer, Bible reading, and meditation. Those habits have disappeared from much of American Christianity. But the distance need not be final. In the busyness of our daily lives, the author suggests adopting a fifteen-, five-, five-program, beginning each day with fifteen minutes of conversation with God, returning to that conversation five times each day, and then concluding with another five minutes before sleep.

Creating and participating in discipleship groups can help. Class meetings were the soul of early Methodism and, for the twenty-first century, should be reintroduced into the religion. The author affirms that spiritual growth will occur in small groups, as it did in Wesley's Holy Club, especially when participants turn attention away from themselves outward to people in need.

Being nurtured in faith calls for discipline. And the author suggests that Methodists and like-minded Protestants should update and re-institute the Wesleyan societies' General Rules of doing no harm, doing good, and keeping the ordinances of faith. Discussing and revising the rules is a task that discipleship groups could take on immediately. But even so, the author insists, revising the General Rules is a task that needs to be addressed at a denominational level. And equally important, clergy should return to the old practice of at least once every year instructing their congregations in the essential responsibilities that accompany discipleship.

Suggestion #2. Let's Give Attention to Understanding the Essential Beliefs, Traditions, and Practices of Our Faith

The author suggests that twenty-first-century Christian churches need to find ways to supplement the learning that traditionally occurred in adult Sunday school classes. While some Sunday school classes for adults today are marvelously effective, too few Christians are involved. Bible studies and short courses of study on Christian theology, history, and ethics can make up some of the deficit. These are best guided by professionals, and it is incumbent for seminary-trained ministers or priests to offer such courses for their congregations.

Clergy should review The Social Principles and other important documents of faith with their congregations. Also, church libraries are underused because they are under-advertised. The catechism of new members provides a wonderful opportunity for significant instruction.

Workshops are possible for some churches and, as with businesses and professional organizations, offering certification and badges of accomplishment can enhance attendance. Success hinges on providing superior quality to presentations along with opportunities for networking and building community. Special opportunity courses and lecture series allow congregations to learn from expert seminary professors or other Christian academic lecturers. Denominational central offices should be called upon to provide financial and logistical support, as needed, for such learning endeavors.

Suggestion #3. Let's Redouble Our Efforts to Be Inclusive

American Christianity's unwillingness to live up to its own affirmations of sisterhood and brotherhood is a sad failure. And the failure reminds the author of the hesitancy, fear, and distrust that occurred in the post-exilic days of the priest Ezra. But other voices like the writers of Ruth and Isaiah 40–66 arose, calling Israel back to its true mission as a light to the nations. Nothing should be clearer, the author affirms, than that Jesus and early Christianity sided with the idea that the one God is Lord over all creation and all peoples.

How to aid American Christianity's search for greater brotherhood and sisterhood? The author suggests that Christians should not be silent in the face of injustice. Solidarity with those who suffer oppression is always the right step—but with the caveat that the methods employed to overcoming prejudice should comport with the example and teachings of Christ. Inclusion and diversity workshops and training can show that minorities are valued and that all of us on occasion are unaware of attitudes we hold or actions we take that hurt others. Much prejudice in society is unintentional and born from ignorance.

The institutional church can model spiritual equality for society. As with learning about the Christian faith, the leadership and planning of workshops, lecture series, discussion groups, and similar diversity and inclusion training in the local church must start with the clergy. But this is a work area also that requires effort at the denominational level. Greater inclusion calls for Christians to leave their comfort zones when it comes to worship.

Suggestion #4. Let's Give Proper Attention to a Christian Philosophy of Living, to Doing Christianity

Perhaps the *Handbook for the Christian Faith*'s most important theme is that true religion can't be separated from the doing of it. Jesus referred to the Pharisees as hypocrites not because they misquoted the Torah, or prayed, or fasted, but because their actions did not comport with their own claims of what God willed.

Sanctification, progressing in thoughts and actions toward greater love of God, other people, and all God's creation is central to a Christian philosophy of living. This philosophy includes understanding that God is God, and we are sons and daughters of God. And it includes progression away from willfully selfish actions. Christians should strive to be useful to God. And they should seek at every turn to love God and their fellow beings. Sanctification is not only a task for individuals but is a work for the church as a body of believers.

As mentioned, the author calls for resurrecting the General Rules of early Methodist class and society meetings. Keeping the ordinances of faith entails rebuilding certain religious habits, spending time on spiritual matters, privately and publicly, as part of a community of faith. When people and churches are led by love, they will strive mightily to do no harm and to do good. People and churches can be models for doing good among believers and society at large.

The author urges that Christian efforts in evangelism should never be deceptive or hateful but should model harmony, kindness, humility, and peace. Missions or Christian outreach, he holds, stands at the core of who we are as Christians. Missions and evangelism need to be conducted differently than even fifty years ago, but their same purpose goes all the way back to the earliest Christians. It is to bring wellness (or salvation, in religious talk) to a broken world.

In sum, a Christian philosophy of living is nothing other than taking Jesus' command to love God and neighbor seriously. Christianity liberates people to love without fear and without compunction of what the world thinks.

Terms, Dates, Events, and People

Define, identify, or explain each word and phrase as they appear in the *Handbook*'s conclusion. Ask your instructor or look up words or phrases that remain unclear.

- aesthetic worship
- agenda for twenty-first-century churches
- the joining of religion and culture in American society
- purpose of worship
- responses to worship
- revival pattern of worship
- traditional worship

Reading Comprehension

Explain these important themes found in the conclusion. Discuss them with course partners. If the *Handbook for the Christian Faith*'s author were in the room with you, what questions would you ask? Can you think of further evidence to buttress the points the author makes?

1. There is strong evidence that Christianity plays a less significant role in the lives of Americans today than fifty years ago. And that is true also

of Christian Americans. The *Handbook*'s author is convinced, however, that a deeper understanding of the essential practices and beliefs of the Christian faith can lead to spiritual and church renewal.

2. The two principal forms of worship current among American Methodists and like-minded Protestants are directed at creating emotional responses among worshipers. L. Edward Phillips identified these two forms of worship as "the revival pattern" and "aesthetic worship," commonly referred to as traditional worship.

3. Sunday school worship and prayer meeting worship have largely vanished from contemporary Methodist churches and American Protestantism in general. That vacuum has increased the difficulty of instructing and nurturing the faith of both children and adults. Anecdotal stories from ministers, nationwide surveys of religious knowledge, denominational membership records, and statistical evidence from church attendance polls show that American Christianity is failing at that task.

4. The author suggests that as a first step to greater spiritual health, American Christians spend more time with God. Such includes building habits of personal holiness, forming and participating in discipleship groups, and for Methodists recapturing and updating the General Rules of early class meetings.

5. As a second step to greater spiritual health, the *Handbook*'s author urges that American Christians give proper attention to learning and understanding essential beliefs, traditions, and practices of historical Christianity. Such includes introducing courses of study into the church calendar, sharing and reviewing the Social Principles and other important documents of the faith, emphasizing catechism, and providing workshops and lectureships for church members.

6. The author suggests as a third step to greater spiritual health that churches redouble efforts to make congregations more inclusive. Appropriating and reaffirming the Christian ideal of brotherhood and sisterhood includes affirming solidarity with those suffering injustices, providing workshops and training for church members as needed, leaving comfort zones behind, and modeling spiritual equality in the local and institutional church.

7. A fourth step to greater spiritual health for American Christians and their local churches is to go beyond confessions of faith to adopting a Christian philosophy of living. The author wants Christians to *do* Christianity. Such includes reemphasizing sanctification (or

progressing on the path to holy living), the importance of keeping the ordinances of faith in personal and public life, doing no harm, and doing good.

8. In a postscript, the author suggests that recapturing the notion of the church as a family of God is of existential importance to Christianity. An ecumenical approach should characterize twenty-first-century American Christianity.

9. The author is convinced that some level of separation from the world and culture is important for Christian identity. But the separation must be of the right kind. Christianity would do well, for example, opposing the choke hold that materialism, money, and power have on American society. As he questioned certain secular values, Jesus offered better alternatives for happiness and fulfillment.

Exercises to Enhance Understanding

1. You have read the *Handbook for the Christian Faith* and are completing the certification course on Spiritual and Church Renewal. Summarize the benefits that have accrued to you through your work.

2. After reflecting on all you have learned, list five things you think important to share with others. Will the information and practices you have learned benefit friends and your church? Can you summarize important information such that it can be shared within a small window of time? If granted a few minutes before your church congregation, Sunday school class, or another group, how might you present some of what you have learned?

3. Using what you have learned in this course, draw up a Spiritual and Church Renewal agenda for your church. How might you discuss, publicize, and enlist others into such a plan for Spiritual and Church Renewal?

Suggested Readings

Harmon, Nolan B., Jr. "Methodist Worship: Practices & Ideals." In *Methodism: A Summary of Basic Information Concerning the Methodist Church*, edited William K. Anderson, 229–39. Nashville: Methodist, 1947.

Matthews, Rex D. *Timetables of History for Students of Methodism*. Nashville: Abingdon, 2007.
Olson, Roger E., et al., eds. *Handbook of Denominations in the United States*. 14th ed. Nashville: Abingdon, 2018.
Phillips, L. Edward. *The Purpose, Pattern and Character of Worship*. Nashville: Abingdon, 2020.

www.ingramcontent.com/pod-product-compliance
Lightning Source LLC
Chambersburg PA
CBHW031500160426
43195CB00010BB/1041